Short Stories **TOKYO SKETCHES**

TOKYO SKETCHES

Short Stories

SKETCHES

Pete Hamill

KODANSHA INTERNATIONAL
Tokyo • New York • London

Distributed in the United States by Kodansha America, Inc.,
114 Fifth Avenue, New York, NY 10011, and in the United Kingdom
and continental Europe by Kodansha Europe Ltd.,
Gillingham House, 38–44 Gillingham Street,
London SW1V 1HU.
Published by Kodansha International Ltd.,
1-17-14 Otowa, Bunkyo-ku, Tokyo 112, and
Kodansha America, Inc.

First edition, 1992
92 93   10 9 8 7 6 5 4 3 2 1

Library of Congress Cataloging-in-Publication Data
Hamill, Pete, 1935–
Tokyo sketches / by Pete Hamill. —1st ed.
p. cm.
ISBN 4-7700-1697-2
1. Tokyo (Japan)—Fiction. 2. Americans—Japan—Tokyo—Fiction
I. Title.
PS3558.A423T64 1992 813'.54—dc20
92-34476 CIP

This book is for
Fukiko

CONTENTS

Notes on Tokyo Sketches   1

A Blues for Yukiko   3

The Price of Everything   15

The Past Is Another Country   29

After the War   41

The Opponent   51

The 48th Ronin   61

The Blue Stone   73

Samurai   85

Running for Home   95

The Magic Word   107

It's Only Rock 'n' Roll   119

Missing in Action   131

Happy New Year   141

Notes on Tokyo Sketches

THESE stories are fragments retrieved from a number of visits I made to Tokyo over the past decade. When I first saw that amazing city, I was overwhelmed by an odd tangle of emotions. Tokyo was at once the most completely foreign town I'd ever seen (though I was the foreigner) and a place that was eerily familiar. Walking alone at night on that first trip, I couldn't read the forest of neon calligraphy. I couldn't read the morning newspapers either, or the nuances of gesture, tone, clothing, attitude—that tight mesh of signs that contain a people. So much of life in Japan is encoded that a stranger could spend a lifetime trying to crack the codes and still fail, because so many codes are continually altered or discarded. In New York, where I was born, I knew most of the codes; and though I couldn't penetrate them in any way, I could identify the codes of Europe. In Tokyo, in those first days, I was looking without seeing.

At the same time, I felt oddly at home. For a New Yorker, Tokyo has the familiar dense vastness of a great city. The basic structures and components are there: rivers, bridges, skyscrapers, traffic, markets, movie houses, parks and subways and bookstores. The streets are as thick with people as the avenues of Manhattan. You hear rap music and rock 'n' roll and the plangent chords of the blues; you see huge crowds filing into baseball stadiums; you see T-shirts from American universities and scarlet caps from the Chicago Bulls. The surface geography of *that* Tokyo is knowable. I could study maps and guidebooks and explore that physical city on foot or by subway. All cities have similar templates. They can be touched, seen, heard, described. Tokyo was no different. Or so I thought.

But as I spent more time in Tokyo—going back with my wife, who was born there, or visiting with newspaper friends—I began hearing stories that convinced me I would always be a stranger in its streets. Our histories are too different, as I understood after listening to many ordinary people who remembered the horrors of World War II and the humiliations of the Occupation. I'm from a city that has never been bombed, a nation that has never been occupied and can't ever fully understand the feelings that accompany such memories. The rubble of the South Bronx might superficially resemble Tokyo in 1945, but self-inflicted wounds aren't the same as wounds inflicted by strangers. To be sure, the Japanese almost never mention the war to visiting Americans. But its immense, almost mythic presence can be felt in those silences.

I also met many Americans who first entered Tokyo *because* of the war, the Occupation, or the later struggles in Korea and Vietnam. They were also silent about the things that happened here when they were young, until you found the moment, usually late at night, to ask the questions that released the tale. All seemed permanently shaped by the past, by unforgiven errors and stupidities and casual brutalities; some were drawn back to Tokyo by the need for redemption or to ease some obscure guilt; others clearly wanted to experience again some ancient careless adventure. Usually, nothing helped, not even whiskey.

Most of these stories originated in some form during those brief encounters late at night. Sometimes the tellers of the tales were Japanese. Sometimes the stories were told about other people. But they often shared some common trait: a broken communication, a misunderstood word, a clash of myths, the enormous, unforgiving power of the past. I thank all those who gave them to me.

Pete Hamill

A Blues for Yukiko

1

When Yukiko Kawasaki arrived by taxi in front of the New Otani Hotel, her hands were damp and trembling. She dried her hands on the velveteen seat, took a breath, paid the fare and then gripped her leather handbag to steady herself. A uniformed man opened the taxi door. But her hands still trembled as she stepped into the hazy late morning light. The great hotel rose above her in a blurred silvery mass; she had never felt smaller or more anonymous. She paused, frozen by nervousness, and longed for a cigarette. All the while thinking: I should not be this nervous. After all, I have done my preparation. I've read all the articles about this man. I've listened to his phonograph records, the new CDs, the old vinyls. I have absorbed the learned discographies of the music scholars. Yes: I am not truly an expert on the blues, but surely I know enough to do this interview.

Even if it is Big Boy Carter.

Even if it is this legend, this blind American master who has returned from decades of obscurity to become a star.

Even if it is my first interview.

She walked quickly into the vast lobby of the New Otani, her high-heeled shoes clacking too loudly (she thought) on the fields of polished stone. The bag was heavy with a tape recorder and extra tapes and two notebooks. She saw a wall filled with clocks that showed the time in all the great cities of the world; she checked her watch, saw that she was a half hour early, and felt her palms leaking again. A half hour was too much time. She wished she could plunge right into the interview, like diving off a board into a frigid swimming pool. Just do it. Get it over with. She glimpsed herself in a mirror and wished, as she had so many times in her twenty years of life, that she was beautiful. There were so many beautiful women in this vast hotel lobby. Shop girls and hotel clerks and translators, all of them walking easily with men, sitting at tables in the open coffee shop, waiting for elevators, lounging on couches: all of them beautiful. Each of them sleek and perfect, with slim bodies and long legs and perfect hair and perfect teeth and perfect eyes shaped like almonds.

Yukiko Kawasaki was certain she was imperfect; her legs too short, her teeth too protrusive, her eyes hidden by thick glasses because she was so nearsighted. She breathed in deeply and thought: well, it will not matter to Big Boy Carter. And then stopped herself, thinking: that is cruel and selfish, a terrible thought, so cold to the man's affliction. Just because I am homely, I should not be relieved that this poor man is blind.

Besides, there were more important worries than her own looks. Starting with the interview itself. There were Westerners everywhere in the hotel, huge men walking in pairs, almost all of them accompanied by one of the perfect women. Those women were translators or interpreters, leading the Westerners to meetings with Japanese businessmen, walking swiftly, with an aura of professional certainty and polished grace. Most of them spoke English, using the language so easily and swiftly that Yukiko could not understand all of what they were saying. Others spoke different languages. French. German. Something that sounded like Japanese, round with vowels, probably Spanish or Italian. And she heard languages that she could not identify at all, could not even guess at, perhaps Russian or the language of Czechoslovakia or some dialect from the Scandinavian countries. How was it that the sleek perfect women spoke even *these* languages? All those melded words made her feel that she was in a room full of radios tuned to different stations.

And she wondered: suppose Big Boy Carter speaks too quickly? Suppose he sits there talking away while the tape recorder unspools and I don't understand? I understand my English-language tapes. I understand movies, when Clint Eastwood or Warren Beatty speak English. But I don't always understand rock-'n'-roll lyrics. Or some black actors. Or Englishmen. Or American athletes I see on television. I certainly don't understand these huge fast-talking men in the lobby.

Her heart began to beat too quickly and she glanced at her watch. It was 11:53. Still seven minutes early. She sat down on one of the couches in the lobby and lit a cigarette. The lighter shook slightly in her hand. She took a deep drag and let the smoke ease out and studied the questions she had written so diligently into her notebook. All the time thinking: I will just ask these questions. They are good questions, even if I don't truly understand the blues. They are intelligent questions. They show knowledge and respect for Big Boy Carter's work. I will ask them. That's all. And he will answer, and if I don't understand, well, I can play the tape later and listen very carefully and play it again and again until I have written down his answers very clearly. Of course. And it doesn't matter if I don't understand the blues either. Everything can be understood later.

Still, Yukiko Kawasaki was anxious. She had been working for less than a year on the music magazine called *Down and Dirty*. During the day, she attended the Tsuda Business School, majoring in English, but after school she went to the magazine for four hours and on Saturdays she was there for ten hours. Sometimes she even brought magazine work home with her, facts to be checked, galleys to be corrected, captions to be written for photographs. As a result, music absorbed more of her energies than school. Popular music. The music listened to by her generation. Rock 'n' roll, reggae, rap (which she absolutely never understood without a lyric sheet in her hands). Her editor, Mr. Ishii, often said that he hired her because she was born on the first day of the great Woodstock Festival in August 1969. Twenty years ago: a lifetime for her, yesterday afternoon for her editor. At the beginning, he assigned her to prepare tea and coffee for the editors and their music world visitors; then she graduated to transcribing English-language interviews and translating them into Japanese; and eventually she started rewriting the scholarly reviews of record albums into Japanese that ordinary human beings could read. Slowly, quietly, with proper shyness and some humor, she began to ask Mr. Ishii to allow her to write some stories on her own. Sometimes he teased her about her grand ambitions. Other times he shrugged. And then three days ago, when Yukiko arrived at the office of *Down and Dirty*, he took her aside near the coffeepot.

"I want you to write an article for us," Mr. Ishii said. "On a blues singer, a living legend named Big Boy Carter. He arrives in Tokyo in three days. And as you know, our blues specialist, Mr. Tachibana, is away at a festival in Montreux. So . . ."

So she was here in the lobby of the New Otani, tamping a cigarette out in the ashtray, suddenly so nervous and runny with panic that she considered going home. Just turning around, hurrying out the door. Past the uniformed doormen and the waiting taxis, and the arriving Western businessmen and the perfect women who awaited them. Passing them all, unseen by any of them, anonymous and private, melting into the hazy sunlight. She saw herself doing all of that, then running to the subway and hiding at home in her room. Forever.

The ease of this thought—its finality—terrified her. She stood up, gathering herself, thinking: No. If I run now, I am finished for life. Ishii-*san* would probably fire me. The others would laugh at me. They would tell their friends on the other magazines and . . . *No!* I must do this. I will do this. I *can* do this. Right now.

Yukiko hurried across the lobby and asked one of the beautiful women where she could find the house phone. In a cool, clipped way, the woman sent her to a row of white telephones on a distant wall. Yukiko asked the operator to connect her to the room of Mr. Carter. There was a pause, then a deep voice.

"Hello?"

Yukiko Kawasaki identified herself and her magazine and heard the man chuckle and say: "Come on up, honey."

2

Big Boy Carter was no longer a boy, of course; various clippings listed his age at sixty-four, sixty-six, and seventy-one, and in one interview he said that he wasn't really sure *how* old he was, since he was born at home and his mother was too busy feeding her thirteen children to bother keeping records. In some *other* interview, he said there were ten children and in another his mother died while bearing him and he and his six sisters and two brothers were raised by his father. Big Boy Carter was a legend; the truth was elusive. But Yukiko immediately saw that part of his name was accurate; he was very big. He filled the door frame as Yukiko stood before him, her eyes level with the second button from the top of his open-necked Hawaiian sports shirt. This rayon garment was a riot of red and green, pink birds and violet palm trees, hanging like a tent outside his slacks but not very successful at hiding the swell of his paunch. Sunglasses masked his useless eyes. His skin was darker than the sunglasses, the darkness emphasized by the pale yellow gleam of his teeth and the white thatch of his fine curly hair, which reminded Yukiko of steel wool. As he stepped aside to let her enter, Yukiko smelled the odor of liquor.

"Hello, there, honey," he said, his voice like rough velvet. "They's some ice over there in a bucket, some drinks, he'p yourself . . . or maybe you'd rather have coffee?"

He spoke slowly, with a purring drawl, but she still missed some of the words. She tried translating them in her head, paging through a mental dictionary, then stopped, responding to the familiar word, *coffee.*

"Yes, coffee, please," she said.

"You mind callin' down for room service?" he said.

"Yes, of course."

Ah, she thought: he can't see the numbers on the telephone. Room service was a simple thing, but not for him. She hit the buttons and ordered in Japanese, all the time watching the large black man in the Hawaiian shirt moving to a massive leather couch, his long delicate fingers brushing the edges of chairs and tables, weaving gracefully through the obstacles. She couldn't see his eyes, of course; but there was a strange fixed grin on his face that she could not decipher. Was he grinning to be pleasant? At his own inadequacies? Or was he smiling in some ironical Western way that she could never understand? Finally he settled into the leather couch, causing a wheezing sound as his large body pushed into the cushions. She knew why they called him Big Boy: even sitting down, he seemed to fill the entire room. Once more, she felt very small.

"That's nice, that Japanese lingo," he said (as she thought: lingo, lingo, what is "lingo"?). "I like the sound of it. Not what I expected it to be, Japanese. Real pretty . . ."

"Thank you," she said. "Thank you."

"Lots of o's and a's," he said, chuckling. "Could write a real smooth song in that lingo . . ."

She sat with her back to the windows, which opened out to the grainy Tokyo skyline. She turned on the tape recorder and laid her list of questions on the low table before her, thinking: *Now*, I must do this *now*. Then there was a knock at the door and she rose, relieved at the postponement, and admitted a young waiter in a white formal jacket and bow tie, carrying a silver coffeepot on a silver tray. "Tha's the coffee, right?" Big Boy Carter said. "Smells good. Let me have three sugars, please, darlin'. And no cream. An' honey you sign the bill, all right?"

Yukiko signed the bill and bowed to the waiter, who bowed in return and eased out of the suite.

"So, you ready, honey?" Big Boy Carter said.

"Yes," she said, wishing her voice were stronger, firmer. "Yes, please, Mister Carter."

"Call me Big Boy. Everybody else do."

"Yes, Mister Big Boy."

Carter chuckled. "Mister Big Boy . . . nobody ever done call me Mister Big Boy before. . . ."

Her heart flipped slightly; she wasn't quite sure what he was saying. She thought: he must speak a special dialect, some form of English spoken in the South. He certainly doesn't speak the King's English as taught at the Tsuda Business School. I must listen carefully, speak clearly, show neither doubt nor fear. Above all, I must go forward. I can't leave unless I finish this task. She knew from her research that Big Boy Carter had grown up poor in the turpentine forests of northern Florida. That was common to all the stories, even the ones where the father, mother and children were a confusion. She asked a question that tried to clear up the confusion, but Big Boy Carter just laughed. "I ain't too sure myse'f," he said. "How many brothers do it *take*? How many sisters? I had one father and one mother. I even remember their faces."

The boy started going blind when he was nine. By the time he was eleven, he'd lost all vision. Yukiko swallowed hard.

"Do you think the blues comes from being poor?" she said.

"Poor got nothin' to do with it," he said in that purring voice, sipping the coffee. "Blues is about bein' *hurt*. Now some people is hurt by bein' poor. But some is not. They just poor, and they accepts it. People gets hurt by lots of other things. By fate, by trouble, by women, . . . Though when I come to think of it, I ain't never heard of no bluesman ever started out rich."

He laughed out loud and put the coffee cup down and reached for his glass. It was standing beside a bottle of Dickel bourbon on the low table that separated him from Yukiko. His delicate hands brushed the bottle and found the glass. The liquid was a pale amber color. If Big Boy used ice, it had melted.

"No, ma'am," he said. "I never heard of no rich blues player . . . young *or* old."

He stopped, as if thinking of something else to say. But then he gave it up and just sipped the watery bourbon. Yukiko looked down at her next question, thinking: I can listen more carefully later, I can get the words exactly right *later*.

"And when you were a boy, when you lost your sight, did that—"

"Hurt?"

She said nothing.

"Yeah, it hurt," he said. "Yeah, it hurt. . . ."

His voice trailed off and he seemed to draw up into himself. Yukiko felt she had made a terrible mistake. How stupid: she never should have asked about his blindness. Not now, at the *beginning* of the interview. How insensitive: to remind him about those years when he still could see the world.

"I'm sorry, Mr. Carter," she said, her voice trembling. "I hope I didn't hurt your feelings by asking about your—"

"My blindness? Oh, hey, honey, don't you be apologizin' now. It ain't your fault. It's a fact of my life, like havin' big feet and black skin. I can't do nothin' about it. It's like some people has freckles. Or a rose is red . . ."

He sipped the bourbon again, and she realized that she could allow her eyes to wander and Big Boy would not think her rude. She noticed that the coffee cup was half full and must be getting cold. She saw his guitar, in a battered case, leaning against a far wall and jotted a note on her pad: his guitar looks sad. As sad as its owner.

"But you know, that reminds me of one time when I was fourteen and just startin' out in the blues life. That was in Biloxi, Mississippi, befo' the war . . ."

So he began to talk, the stories flowing from him like a river, words Yukiko understood and words she didn't, as he told the tale of his life in the blues. For more than an hour, sipping the bourbon, he talked about mornings in Texas, and bad food in Alabama, and evil nights in Chicago. He talked about a stabbing in New Orleans and the time he did in a Georgia jail—for pissing on a sidewalk at three in the morning. He talked about women and wives (four of them) and agents who stole his money and rock 'n' rollers who stole his licks.

Yukiko was thrilled: it was like a song. He talked about his come-back too and how the whole thing started the year before when that damn crazy white boy came and found him in Shreveport. He was long retired, long forgotten, didn't even have some of his own records, living in a damn ten-dollar-a-week boardinghouse on social security. And that damn crazy white boy came and talked to him and brought him to a recording studio and set up a table with sandwiches and bourbon and got him to sing the blues. After that, he was on television on a late-night show (*Arsenio, you ever see Arsenio here in Japan?*) and Mick Jagger saw him and called him at the studio and then gave an interview about him to *Rolling Stone*, the magazine they all read, and, well, it was like a miracle, like a god-damned miracle.

Big Boy Carter told all of this with almost no prompting from Yukiko. And, more important to her, he told it with a singular lack of bitterness; he even seemed delighted about some of the dreadful things he had survived. And then he leaned back exhausted, the words running down, and sat there in silence. The odd grin was gone, and for a moment, Yukiko wondered if Big Boy Carter had fallen asleep. He hadn't.

"Tell me," he said quietly. "On the other side of the window, what's out there?"

She smiled. "Tokyo," she said. "Just Tokyo."

"No, there gotta be more than that. Tell me what you *see* out there."

She switched off the tape recorder and went to the window. She looked down at a thousand rooftops spread out below her in the midday haze. She had never seen her native city from this great height and she was startled.

"Many buildings," she said, self-conscious about her English, wishing she could use Japanese, never sure when she was speaking English where she should place the articles, "a" and "the" and "an," and choosing to leave most of them out. In a formal interview, she would write them out; now, she wasn't sure. She just talked, saying the words. "Rooftops. Advertising signs. Oh, and Emperor's Palace. It is in large park and trees are very green. You can see . . . I think in English it is called, uh, *moat?* Full of water, very green. And birds! I can see birds. Thousands of birds, flying in sky. They look like . . . like cloud, dark cloud, moving . . . on sky."

"Birds," Big Boy Carter said. "I used to love lookin' at birds. . . . What else is down there?"

"Now, down on roof, over to right, woman with red dress. Putting laundry on clothesline. She stops, she looks at birds too. And . . . wait: man comes on roof. Young man. Wearing white shirt. He waits at roof door. And now he comes to her. And he, he . . . oh! . . . he *kisses* her."

"Yeah," Big Boy Carter said. "Yeah, I like that. That's sweet."

"But wait. She turns away from him. His arms are folded. Like this." Yukiko started to demonstrate the way the man's arms were folded then stopped, her face flushing. "Across his chest. Folded. Woman, she . . . she is crying. She puts hand to her face."

"Oh, man," Big Boy Carter said. "And what's *he* doing?"

"Very sad. He stands near her, arms down now, but afraid to go to her. Very sad. He says something. She does not answer. Now, oh now, oh how *sad*, now he turns away. He *leaves*." She stopped talking for a long moment. "She is alone now. Crying very hard."

The room was quiet for a long moment. Then Big Boy Carter said in a whisper:

"You see, everybody know the blues."

3

When she turned from the window, Big Boy Carter was standing. She looked at him, wondering what he thought now, and whether his thoughts were words or music or some special combination of both. He stepped toward her.

"Excuse me," he said. "Do you mind? I don't know what you look like."

Delicately, he touched her face with both hands.

"I knew it," he said. "You're beautiful."

"Oh, no," she said, embarrassed, but not moving, afraid that if she pulled away she would hurt his feelings. "No, Mister Big Boy, I'm not beautiful. There are many beautiful women in Tokyo but—"

"You're beautiful," he insisted, his huge fingers gently touching her brow, her cheekbones, her nose, her chin.

She was suddenly afraid. Of his size and his fame and of what he might think of her. *Perhaps he thinks I am some girl sent here for him. Or he thinks I am like those girls in America that we have written about in the magazine. What is the word? Women who follow musicians around to sleep with them? Groupie. Yes. Groupie. Perhaps—*

Then he touched her neck.

And she ducked away.

"I must go," she said.

"You finished with the interview?" he said, his face looking baffled.

"No, I have many more questions, but I—"

"Then stay," he said. "Please don't go."

"I— I can't," she said, and then lied: "I have other appointment. Other . . . interview."

She reached for her tape recorder, picked it up, turned abruptly, and eased around behind a chair. Her heart was thumping. Big Boy Carter was a large dark silhouette now against the pale light of the window. His brow was furrowed in what might be anger.

"I'm sorry," he said in a flat, remote voice. "I scared you. You afraid, ain't you, girl? I can smell it off you. Fear got a smell, if you know how to smell it. And I put some fear in you, didn't I?"

"No, it's . . ."

She tried to find the correct English words, words that would express her departure as politely as possible. But the words bounced around, colliding with each other in her mind, and she gave up.

"I must go," she said.

She started for the door, and then turned. Big Boy was in the same place. He was very still, his head bowed now, and she could see that he was struggling for control, breathing deeply, his hands opening and closing.

He looked suddenly very old, and at the same time, quite young. As still as a statue. Like a monument to his own life: the old man who'd been rediscovered too late was combined in that hurting figure with the young boy who once saw birds and flowers and skies.

She paused at the door, her fingers touching its handle. And thought: I want to hold him and keep him from crying. I want to take him to bed and tell him that his hurt has finally ended. I want to hear him tell me that I'm beautiful. Just once again, before I leave.

"I guess you better go," he said hoarsely. "I didn't mean nothin' . . . but, hey, go on now, honey."

She searched for words in English that would express her sorrow. Again, they would not come.

All she could say was, "Thank you, Mister Big Boy."

"Yeah," he whispered. "God bless."

Then she went out, closing the door softly behind her, and took the elevator down to the world of perfect women with perfect teeth and huge men who spoke quickly in English and uniformed doormen who never saw the birds in the Tokyo sky. She didn't look back at the hotel. She lit a cigarette, smoking greedily as she walked. And when she reached the subway, blind from the tears that filled her eyes, she thought she was beginning to understand the blues.

The Price of Everything

1

Mr. Ishimoto met Mr. Spence on the steps of the Metropolitan Museum on a fiercely hot day in August. Their encounter was a matter of Mr. Ishimoto's need and Mr. Spence's availability. Mr. Ishimoto needed a light for his cigarette. Mr. Spence produced a lighter.

"Are you here to see the Cézanne show?" Mr. Spence asked.

Mr. Ishimoto did not quite understand. He actually wanted only to smoke a cigarette and then use the men's room, because on his morning constitutional from the Carlyle Hotel, he had found no public urinal in this strange hot city. He nodded his head, yes.

"Well," Mr. Spence said with a smile, "we'll go together."

And so they did. They took some hurried drags on their respective cigarettes and then went in. They were an odd couple. Mr. Ishimoto was short and stocky, with a gnarled face that looked like a fist. Below his knuckled brow, thick glasses seemed welded to his short blunt nose and his mouth was a tense tough slit. At that first meeting, he was sixty-two years old, a veteran of the Pacific War, a widower without children; he was worth seventeen million dollars. Mr. Spence was six-foot-three, with lean, magazine model good looks. His face was an assembly of smooth planes. His teeth were even and white. His stomach was flat. He had served in no wars, had never been married, and had exactly $311 in his bank account. They had only one thing in common: each wore a blue blazer from Brooks Brothers. Mr. Ishimoto had purchased his in Tokyo, in preparation for his first trip to New York. Mr. Spence had bought his in the old Madison Avenue shop three years earlier and the lining of the pockets was beginning to fray from use.

Together, they wandered through the marble distances of the galleries, with Mr. Spence providing the commentary. Mr. Ishimoto didn't understand why these pictures were considered so important, even after Mr. Spence had enlisted the services of a wandering Japanese art student to serve as translator. Mr. Spence, in fact, described the paintings with words that Mr. Ishimoto had never heard before and could never remember later. Mr. Ishimoto looked at a perfectly ordinary landscape, with some sloppy paint applied very thickly, and Mr. Spence talked about the history of cubism, the geometries of the design, the shallow space of the picture plane. Mr. Ishimoto thought this was pure nonsense, but he did not want to seem rude; he nodded politely, as if he understood. When they were finished, and the student had wandered off to another floor, they emerged from the air-conditioned museum into the thick damp New York heat. Mr. Ishimoto took another light from Mr. Spence's lighter. Mr. Spence handed him a business card, which identified him as the president of Spence Art Services Ltd. And Mr. Ishimoto gave Mr. Spence his own card, which, alas, was in Japanese.

They were about to leave, awkwardly bowing and shaking hands at the same time, when a tour bus pulled up at the curb and a group of Japanese visitors began to emerge. A young Japanese woman was in charge, speaking quickly and politely to the group, telling the driver in perfect English that they would be finished in exactly one hour. Mr. Spence approached her.

"Excuse me, ma'am," he said, "but you speak Japanese, do you not?"

"Yes, I do," she said, smiling a dazzling smile.

"Could you do me a favor?" he said. "Would you tell this gentleman that if he ever needs to buy paintings, he can call me, or write me at my gallery?"

"Of course."

The young woman spoke rapidly in Japanese to Mr. Ishimoto,

explaining that Mr. Spence was an art dealer and could be reached at the address on the business card. Mr. Ishimoto nodded, looked again at the tall American's card, and bowed solemnly. When he looked up, the woman was walking away. Mr. Ishimoto thought that he'd never seen a woman so beautiful.

2

Mr. Ishimoto saw the young woman again seven months later in Tokyo. The occasion was a small trade show for which Mr. Ishimoto's tool-and-die company had organized a booth. The show opened with a cocktail party, and Mr. Ishimoto stood with his vice presidents and his assistants and his marketing men and ignored the babble of languages in the room. He had been to a hundred similar events in his lifetime and they were all the same: boring to the point of numbness.

Then the widower saw the woman. The beautiful young woman with the dazzling smile. The one he'd glimpsed so briefly on the steps of the Metropolitan Museum in New York.

She was in a mixed group of Japanese and Americans, obviously translating for them, dressed in a neatly cut lavender suit and high heels that made her seem even taller. Mr. Ishimoto stopped a waiter, took a Scotch and soda, lit a Mild Seven and casually moved over to the group for which the woman was translating. He stood on the fringe and half-listened. They talked about the dollar and the yen, about import and export licenses, about the quality of Taiwanese steel, about a lot of other things.

But Mr. Ishimoto cared little for any of that. He was looking at the woman's creamy skin, at her lustrous hair, at the curve of her hip under the severe and proper cut of her skirt. Her voice was low and evenly modulated but she seemed relaxed with the language of the Americans. In fact, Mr. Ishimoto thought, she sounded like all those American actresses he had seen in the movies after the war: Deanna Durbin, Maureen O'Hara, and that other one, what was her name?

The one who later married so many men? Elizabeth Taylor. Yes, this woman's voice was like theirs when she spoke English. Liquid. Smooth.

He sipped his Scotch and lit another cigarette. An American told a joke and the other Americans laughed while the young woman translated, and then the Japanese laughed. She smiled politely, obviously thinking it was not much of a joke. Mr. Ishimoto agreed. And then the group began to disperse, with an exchange of name cards, bows, handshakes, the young woman smiling and talking in several languages. Mr. Ishimoto waited. And then faced her.

"I wonder if you remember me," he said.

She paused, as if mentally going through a file, and not finding the card.

"New York," he said. "You brought a group of tourists to the museum . . ."

"Yes, yes," she said, her face brightening. "Yes, I remember."

3

Her name was Yumiko Watanabe. She gave him her name card and he called her twice to interpret for him at meetings with visiting Americans. He didn't truly need her; there were two men on his staff who spoke excellent English. But he wanted to see her. And the more he saw her, the more intoxicated he became. She was not married and lived alone in an apartment in a new building in Aoyama. When she came to interpret the third time, he invited her to stay for lunch in the executive dining room. She smiled and agreed, and as they dined, he began to learn more about her. She was thirty years old and had gone to college in America, to a school in a place called Utah, where she studied art history with, as she said, a minor in literature. Her mother lived in western Japan. Her father was dead. She was an only child.

At night after that, alone in his old house in Kanda, Mr. Ishimoto thought about her constantly. He had been alone now for almost six years, and in the last eight years of his marriage, his wife had been terribly ill. It had been so long since he'd felt a woman beside him in the night, had touched a woman's naked flesh or heard a woman's murmurous voice. He was never a man who could go with prostitutes, not even when he was young, not even in the army in Taiwan when his friends would go off and get drunk on rice wine and sleep with the whores. He was too proud for that. And for Mr. Ishimoto, his pride was everything, although he was not vain. After the war, he'd arrived in the ruins of Tokyo with three yen in his pockets and holes in his shoes and now . . . No, his pride could not allow him now, as he grew old, to pay for sex.

But love was another matter. When his wife had died at last, he felt no emotion except relief; she had been sick for so long, and his own grief had been burned out early in the illness. But when she was gone, he had removed all traces of her from the house. Her clothes and shoes, all photographs, even letters he'd saved from the war: all were taken to storage. An old woman came each day to clean, to make certain that he had coffee in the morning, that his clothes were cleaned and the laundry done. But in the house now, it was as if his wife had never existed. This erasure was an act of will; he knew that. An attempt to erase the past, to remove anything that would dissolve him into tears.

But now, once again, he wanted to hear the creak of a board under a woman's foot as she moved through the rooms. He wanted to see, in the fine Western bathroom, the creams and lotions and mysterious powders that women brought with them. He wanted to see a woman's clothes in the closets and a woman's shoes, lined up neatly on the floor, like oddly shaped weapons. And he wanted in his life, for these final years, to hear the soft, liquid, musical voice of a woman in these rooms that had for too long been frozen into solitude.

One morning, tense and nervous, he called Yumiko and asked her to dinner. She agreed. They went to an expensive Chinese restaurant in Shinjuku. She seemed slightly uncomfortable, as if afraid that others would think she was his mistress. He thought this understandable; he was uncomfortable himself, realizing that he was more than thirty years older than she was, and could easily be her father. So he was publicly quite correct. Even formal. And when he dropped her off that night, the formality persisted. At home alone, he imagined her thinking of him as a stiff, inflexible old man. He did not fall asleep until four in the morning.

4

He was in his office when Mr. Spence called from New York. On an extension, Mr. Spence had arranged for a translator, a male with a sing-song voice, who spoke Japanese with a strange accent.

"I called to see if you might be interested in some artwork," Mr. Spence said. "I remember how engrossed you were in New York last year."

Mr. Ishimoto was polite, remembering the tall American, remembering his own discomfort that day and how he was not at all impressed with the paintings. But he said yes, certainly, I'm always interested in art. Mr. Spence talked about art as the greatest of all financial investments, and Mr. Ishimoto remembered reading some article in one of the monthlies saying the same thing. And Mr. Spence said he would send along some slides. They promised each other to stay in touch. And Mr. Ishimoto went back to work.

It turned out to be a day of immense and complicated problems. There were continuous meetings because the Americans had decided to devalue the dollar in an attempt to compete with the Japanese and reduce their terrible trade deficit. Mr. Ishimoto's experts presented scenarios for the worst case: a collapse of the business. Others talked about cutting back on personnel. Some said the stock market would collapse. Mr. Ishimoto listened. And when the long day was over, he knew that the value of his company had doubled, that he was now wealthy beyond all of his dreams.

At home that night, exhausted, feeling old, he wondered what he could ever possibly do with so much money. He had no heir. His wife's sadness had been rooted in that accident. She was barren and blamed herself all those years. But he'd stayed with her. He had to: she had stayed with him, through the long absences of the war, through the worst of the Occupation, through all the years when Mr. Ishimoto was poor. But after a life with her, he had no son. He had no daughter. And now he had no wife.

He said the word into the emptiness. *Wife.* And the image of Yumiko flowered again in his exhausted imagination. This time, he imagined her in the dim light of the room, coming to his bed. He whispered her name out loud. *Yumiko.* And again. Until he fell at last into a troubled sleep.

5

They had dinner twice more in the new restaurants of a Tokyo that Mr. Ishimoto didn't really know: Italian food and French food, and waiters with gloves. He maintained his formality, but she told him the latest jokes about politicians and other businessmen, and Mr. Ishimoto laughed too loud and then worried that in laughing he would look to her like just another old man with crooked teeth. But he told her some jokes too, old ones, jokes learned in the army, jokes from the fifties, all cleaned up for his audience of one. The jokes were so old that for Yumiko they were new, and she laughed at them, and Mr. Ishimoto felt better. Laughter, after all, was a kind of intimacy.

He used her again as an interpreter with a major client, so that she would know how large his business was, and noticed how comfortable she had become, as if she were a part of his company and not simply hired for the day. He paid her too much, and the accountant pointed this out to him, but he waved a hand and said, "It's all right, she's the best in Tokyo."

And then she invited him to a small dinner party at her own apartment. He prepared for this diligently. A new suit, a bright tie so that he would not look so grave, new shoes. He read the newspapers carefully, so that he would be up on all the latest developments and could discuss them with intelligence. In the afternoon, he walked to a bookstore and tried to find some books of jokes, so that, if necessary, he could tell a joke that was not forty years old. He tried to nap but was too nervous.

He had a chauffeur now and a large car and as he was driven through the clotted Tokyo traffic that evening, he felt increasingly inadequate and worried about looking foolish. He had brought some gifts: a bottle of sake, some traditional rice cakes, a lovely single iris. He reminded himself of his stature in the business world. But when he came to her door on the seventh floor, he was almost incapable of speech. She was wearing a black formal dress, pearls, small earrings. She had never looked so beautiful.

He went in, was introduced to another couple, and immediately forgot their names. The man was a professor of American literature who, like Yumiko, had studied in the States. The woman was an executive at one of the major hotels. They talked about some new books, which were unknown to Mr. Ishimoto. He listened. He nodded. But his eyes were searching the small apartment for clues to the character of this young woman, this Yumiko. There were many bookshelves, crammed with thick, heavy books about art. There was a new machine for playing CDs and cassettes, and shelves full of both. There were pictures on all of the walls, some of them small framed drawings, some watercolors, the others large framed posters from museums or art galleries. He had read some of the names in newspapers and magazines: Picasso and Monet and van Gogh. Others he did not know at all.

Then, out of politeness, Yumiko shifted the conversation away from books and on to business. And Mr. Ishimoto felt more confident. He talked about trade and the Americans and the coming competition from a united Europe. He talked about investments in real estate. He talked about supercomputers and high-definition television. And the younger people listened. They asked intelligent questions, all through dinner. They even made jokes and Mr. Ishimoto told his new ones, learned from the book, and was pleased and astonished when the younger people laughed. He sipped some sake. He asked for Scotch, which he much preferred, and Yumiko brought a bottle from another room and they each had a drink. Mr. Ishimoto told them that he was still uneasy in high buildings and someone said that they were only on the seventh floor and Mr. Ishimoto said yes, I know, but there are thirty more stories above us and they could all go over together. They smiled, but he reminded them that he was born during the time of the great earthquake that destroyed Tokyo. The young professor said that modern architects erected buildings that don't collapse and his wife said that was what they said in Mexico City too and Yumiko laughed in a nervous way.

Then the evening was over. And as they started to say their good-byes, Mr. Ishimoto paused to look at one of the posters. Yumiko noticed his interest and came over.

"Which is your favorite?" he said.

"Of the modern painters?"

"Yes."

She smiled and her brow furrowed and she shrugged and said: "I suppose Picasso. It's a cliché, but, yes, Picasso."

"Why?"

This time she laughed in a teasing way. "Perhaps because he was still going strong at ninety."

The next day, Mr. Ishimoto telephoned Mr. Spence.

6

A Picasso? Of course, but it would take some time. What period? Ishimoto didn't know anything about "periods." He said: "The best period." Yes, Mr. Spence said, of course.

Meanwhile, Mr. Ishimoto had begun to change his life. He went to the eye doctor and replaced his thick glasses with contact lenses. For the first week he dreaded inserting them, but slowly the process became easier and besides, everyone agreed that the lenses made him look younger. He went on a diet and joined a gymnasium near his office and began to lose the thickness around his belly. He tried to stop smoking cigarettes and failed, but he did give up Scotch. When he had lost almost four kilos, his clothes began to look baggy; he went to a new tailor and bought ten new suits and added some new shoes. In the limousine, he asked the chauffeur to play the most popular radio station so that he could hear the new music. The chauffeur looked at Mr. Ishimoto as if he were losing his grip, but the chauffeur did what he was asked to do, and Mr. Ishimoto diligently tried to make sense of rap music. The chauffeur didn't understand it either.

All of this, of course, was for Yumiko. She seemed delighted. She bought him some brighter ties to go with his new suits. She admired his shoes. She marveled at how trim he looked. One summer night, leaving a restaurant together, she took his arm and held it tightly, warmly, affectionately. And because he did not want her to let go of him, he began to walk with her, block after block, with the chauffeur following in the limousine at a discreet distance. He noticed that she was looking at him now in a different way, as if trying to decide whether this much older man was serious. And she seemed to understand that he was.

But Mr. Ishimoto never said the words. He could never say, "I love you." A man of his generation couldn't say such words. They were for movies or songs. And he never suggested marriage. The reason was simple: he was afraid. If she said no, he would be crushed. And he was too old for a defeat. So he postponed all of that and saw her as often as he could. He sent a rose to her house each morning. He brought albums of music to her. But he was very careful about his gifts; he did not want her to think of him as a rich old man trying to purchase a beautiful young woman. When she had to take a group to Hawaii for a week, he swallowed his jealousy and telephoned her each day, no longer chatting about trade or the Americans or a united Europe, but making small talk, about the

weather, and things he'd seen on television and once, to her aston-
ishment, even mentioning the words of a Japanese heavy metal
group he'd seen on television. On one of those nights, when he
called and she was not in her room, he imagined her dancing with
some tall and handsome young man and he could not sleep.

Three weeks after she returned from Hawaii, he heard from Mr.
Spence.

The American had located a Picasso from the best period. But
it was very expensive. How expensive? Mr. Spence cleared his
throat and told Mr. Ishimoto that the asking price was three million
dollars.

Mr. Ishimoto paused, and Mr. Spence moved in to break the
silence. "I've sent you slides," he said. "Federal Express. So you can
see what I mean. Personally," the American said, his voice becoming
icy and superior, "I think it's a very great painting. From the best
period. And the price is *very* low."

The slides were on Mr. Ishimoto's desk the next day. He held
them up to the light, peering at them, the painting shown full-
length, in close-up, in detail. Mr. Ishimoto thought it was a nice
painting, of a very thin young man in what seemed to be a circus
costume. But three million dollars? When he came back from the
war, there wasn't three million dollars in all of Tokyo. His ancestors
to the beginning of time, every one of them combined, had not
earned a total of three million dollars. It was absurd. Mr. Ishimoto
thought: I might spend such a sum on a nice medium-sized hotel in
a nice medium-sized town; but on a painting? He considered calling
in an expert, someone who could tell him the value of the painting.
But that might call attention to it; if the price was indeed a bargain,
then someone else might discover that the painting was available.
He could lose it.

That night, alone in bed, he thought about Yumiko again, as he
always did now in the hour before sleep. The next morning, he
cabled Mr. Spence his agreement to buy the Picasso.

7

The money was sent, a cash transfer from Mr. Ishimoto's bank to the bank of Mr. Spence. The painting arrived two days later, in a huge packing crate. It took three of Mr. Ishimoto's maintenance men an hour to open the crate. The elegantly framed painting was brought to Mr. Ishimoto's office and he sat alone for a long time gazing at it, thinking: Yes, it was a splendid painting. Yes, it was worth the price.

He had his secretary wrap the painting in handmade paper and then called Yumiko, telling her he had to see her that evening. It was important. She said she would be working with some Americans early in the evening, but if it was really so important, he could come to the apartment around ten.

He arrived in the limousine ten minutes early. Sitting alone in the dark back seat, he rehearsed the words he would say to her, shaping them first this way and then that way, trying to imagine what she would say and then what he would say in reply. His body was tense; he felt the way he did early in his career, when making a decision that could move the company forward to another level or lead to complete and utter failure. At one minute to ten, he told the chauffeur to wait, stepped out of the car, and entered the lobby of her apartment house. He rang the bell. But there was no answer. He tried again. Still no answer. He returned to the limousine and used the car phone to call her number, a number that he now knew by heart. He got her answering machine, and hung up. Well, he thought, I will wait.

She arrived in a taxi at ten minutes to eleven. She apologized in a way that struck him as sincere; the Americans talked and talked, and she had no way to call him for she didn't know the number in his car. Mr. Ishimoto looked unperturbed. She invited him upstairs for tea. He nodded to his driver, who opened the trunk and lifted out the beautifully wrapped painting.

"What's this?" she said, smiling.

"For you," he said. "A surprise."

One of the secretaries had ingeniously attached a silk rope handle to the outside of the package and Mr. Ishimoto carried it across the lobby and into the elevator. He glanced at Yumiko and she gave him a curious look. He felt as if everything was now moving in slow motion. They got off on her floor. They walked down the corridor. She took her keys from her handbag. She inserted a key in the lock. She turned the key. She opened the door. Mr. Ishimoto's heart was pounding so hard he was afraid she could hear it.

Then he was on the couch and she was in the kitchen, preparing tea. After a few minutes, she came to him and smiled and said, "Well, what is the big surprise?"

For a second that seemed to him much longer, he hesitated, thinking *I am an old man, so please do not laugh.* Then he asked her to sit beside him. And he let the words pour out. How knowing her had changed his life, how he felt his long loneliness was at an end, how he needed her and wanted her. He said he knew that she was young and he was old, that she was in the May of her life and he was in November. But he said that he was certain that such a difference would not matter too greatly. He would be kind to her, he would take care of her, and she could take care of him.

When he finished, he turned to look at her. And saw that she had a hand to her face and her eyes were glistening.

"You are a very sweet man," she whispered.

He didn't know what she meant. So he stood up and took the wrapped painting and handed it to her.

"For you," he said. "Perhaps for us."

Carefully, almost delicately, she began to open the package. And then saw the painting. The Picasso. The tints of rose and pale blue were muted in the dim light of the lamp beside her. She ran her fingertips over its surface. She brought it close to her face, as if to inhale its odor, perhaps even (Mr. Ishimoto thought) to kiss it.

"It's beautiful," she said.

"Yes," he said. "And so are you."

She looked at him, at his lumpy face, his need, his desire to please her. And then she turned away and buried her face in the pillows of the couch and began to cry. Deep, inconsolable sobs made her body heave and fall. Mr. Ishimoto didn't know what to do. He sat frozen for a long moment and then put his arm around her. She burrowed her head against his chest and continued to weep. He held her very tightly, and spoke old words, words he had spoken to nobody in many years, crooning words he'd heard from his mother in a Japan that no longer existed.

Until finally she whispered to him.

"Yes," she said. "I'll be your woman . . ."

And she looked past him, across the room, at the book that contained this same Picasso painting, the real one that was hanging on the wall of the Louvre.

"You are such a kind man," she said, thinking: I cannot hurt you with the truth. Thinking: tomorrow I must hide that book forever. Then she took his face in her tapered fingers and said again: "You are so very kind . . ."

The Past Is Another Country

1

As the giant airplane began its long, gradual descent into Tokyo, George Walker began to feel uneasy. The reason wasn't clear; after all, he was returning to a city in which he had once been twenty-one. Maybe that was the problem; more than forty years had passed, an entire lifetime. A wife had lived most of those years with him and then been taken to a graveyard; children had been born, learned to walk and talk, started schools and graduated, married and finally gone off. And for himself, a career had begun, blossomed, matured, and then faded. He had little to add to any of it. Coming now to Tokyo for the second time, he carried almost as little baggage as he had on that first journey, long ago.

Still, even understanding the lightness of his own ambition, he did not feel footloose or free. Gazing around the cabin at the Japanese businessmen stirring out of slumber, staring for a moment at the pretty stewardesses, still as crisp and efficient as they had been when they departed New York many hours earlier, watching a videotaped explanation of customs and passport control, George Walker was seized with a feeling of loneliness. There were almost no other Americans on the airplane. When he left Japan in 1947, Tokyo was still digging out of the rubble of the firebombings; MacArthur still reigned in imperial splendor at his fabled GHQ; and the United States was the greatest military and economic power on earth. On that first trip, Walker arrived with the swagger of a conqueror. For a generation after that, Americans swaggered around the earth, filling the seats on the night flights, speaking with the authority of success.

Now everything had changed. Without firing a shot, Japan had become a major world power, the conquerors had been conquered, and George Walker could not remember a single word of the crude Japanese he'd learned when he was a raw young man. My memory is gone, he thought. I can't even remember last month.

A cool feminine voice instructed him in English to fasten his seat belt in preparation for landing and then repeated the message in Japanese. George Walker closed his eyes. He began to see jagged images of the Japan he'd left: rubble, hungry men, bitter women and . . . He opened his eyes to kill the images and then, almost as an act of reassurance, to prove to himself that this journey wasn't all illusion, he removed the letter from his jacket pocket. The letter that had put him on this airplane. The letter that told him in simple English that he was invited to come to Japan to discuss possible investment in Walker's machine tool business in Ohio. When he first read those words, he had laughed out loud. The American machine tool business had been destroyed by the Japanese—and now they wanted to invest in it? The irony was too heavy; he suspected a joke on the part of one of his friends. In the past decade, the Japanese had even made him cry, as all the old certainties of his business collapsed around him; now, with words out of nowhere, they had made him laugh.

But sitting in his dusty office in Cleveland, staring at the letterhead of Inoya Enterprises, reading the plain and tempting language of the invitation, he began to feel an emotion that had left him years before: hope. Maybe it was no joke. Maybe he *should* go to Japan, persuade the Japanese—or at any rate, *this* Japanese—to invest millions in the old Walker shop and guarantee him a certain amount of business. Then Walker could pay off the old debts, square himself with the tax people, call good old Harry Majewski back from retirement in Florida to run the shop, hire some young guys from the collapsing plants of Detroit, . . . Hell (George Walker had said out loud, in the empty office in Cleveland), I could get back into *production*! I could build up the Walker *name* again! I could maybe even sell the whole goddamned business to the Japanese, take the money and *run!* Retire in Mexico or some place! Hawaii! And all those people that looked at me like I had some fatal *disease* . . . even my own *kids*: they'd have to treat me with *respect* again, call me *Mister* Walker again, instead of Poor George, come home at Christmas, slap me on the back, treat me like my goddamned life *meant* something.

So he called the number in Tokyo and it was no joke. He talked with a young woman who spoke crisp, British-accented English, arranged the date, was told that two days later a pre-paid ticket in his name would be at Japan Air Lines in New York. He told no one that he was leaving; in truth, nobody cared. He packed a bag, took a bus to New York (to save money) and now, here he was, coming down into a city in which he once was young.

The uneasiness did not go away.

2

When George Walker cleared customs and passport control and came out into the terminal carrying his bag, the young woman was waiting for him, holding a handsomely lettered placard bearing his name. Her face was a pale wedge, her eyes masked behind tinted glasses. The shoulders of her jacket were padded. The effect was efficient and severe.

"Hello," he said. "I'm George Walker."

"Hello," she said. "Welcome to Tokyo. I am Miss Kubota." She turned to a small uniformed man and spoke in Japanese. The man took Walker's bag, and then Miss Kubota led the way outside, past lines of taxis and private cars and policemen with blank faces. They stopped at a silver Mercedes-Benz. The uniformed man opened the trunk and placed the bag inside, and then came around and opened the back door for Walker.

"The driver will take you to Mr. Inoya's house," Miss Kubota said. "It is a long way, but Mr. Inoya thought you would be more comfortable than in Tokyo, with all of its noise. If you are hungry, there is some lunch in the small compartment there, and some iced drinks. Have a nice trip."

She said all of this as if giving orders, but George Walker was too tired to protest. If anything, he was relieved that he was not going into the heart of Tokyo. Miss Kubota bowed, Walker bowed in return and then got into the Mercedes.

He sat back, but could not tell where he was going. He saw Japanese soldiers at the airport gates, but they did not stop the Mercedes. The chauffeur drove on smoothly, silently, passing a long stretch of factory buildings that looked like downtown Cleveland. Walker saw signs in the calligraphic script that he remembered from his youth but could not read; again, they made him feel illiterate. The traffic thickened and slowed. He struggled against a heavy drowsiness. He leaned back, trying to think of words to say to his Japanese host, words of persuasion, words about the glittering future of the machine tool business. In fragments and incomplete phrases, he made a case for investment. He prepared a speech about quality control. He conjured a plan for supplying machined parts to the Honda plant in Youngstown. But the effort soon exhausted him and he fell into a dreamless sleep.

3

When he awoke, the world was dark. The chauffeur pulled the Mercedes into a gravel driveway leading to a large modern house and then stopped. The man got out and opened the door of the car, bowing to Walker and offering him a gloved hand. Walker ignored the hand and stepped outside. The air was thinner here, crisper, with many stars. He knew he must be in the mountains. Off to his left, he could see a distant glow in the sky: Tokyo. The chauffeur lifted the suitcase and led the way up the stairs to the main entrance, stopping before a wide oak door. He said nothing, did not knock, rang no bell. But the door opened and a middle-aged woman appeared, bowing to Walker, saying something in Japanese. She was dressed in a white silk kimono, her hair piled up the way Japanese women appeared in old woodcuts.

Behind her was a spacious living room, elegantly furnished, the living room, George Walker thought, of a successful businessman. But there was no businessman. There was nobody here except this middle-aged woman. She gestured to him to remove his shoes and don slippers. He felt self-conscious doing this, afraid that his feet might carry the odor of the long flight. But he unlaced the shoes, standing clumsily on one leg, then wriggled into the slippers, which were too small for his wide American feet. The woman waited patiently, showing neither amusement nor disdain. Then she moved her head, indicating to Walker that he should follow her. The slippers made a scuffing sound as he moved behind her, afraid to lift his feet in his usual way because the slippers would fall off. They went down a corridor, past closed doors, past framed lithographs and paintings and small tables adorned with elegant bowls. The woman stopped at the final door, opened it, showed him in.

There was a large bed, covered with a pale yellow spread. An envelope lay on the pillow. She lifted the envelope, gave it to him, bowing, he thought, as if it were an offering. In her presence, an old feeling came back to Walker. As he had in Japan when he was young, he felt clumsy again, too large, too fat, devoid of all grace. "Thank you," he said in English. "Thank you."

She showed him the small door opening on a bathroom, tapped a finger on a ceramic carafe of water, slid open the dresser drawers. All of this was done swiftly, efficiently, as if ritual, and then she bowed once more, backed out of the room and was gone. George Walker breathed deeply, then lifted the envelope and opened it. There was a note inside.

Dear Mr. Walker, it said in handwritten English. *I will be a little late. Please forgive me. Since you must have jet lag, I suggest you nap a while and we can have a late supper.* It was signed with the letter "*I.*"

He sat on the edge of the bed and gazed at the single page in a baffled way.

4

It was very late—probably long after midnight—when the woman led Walker down the corridor again, past the living room and into a dining room. Here at last was his Japanese host. The man was standing near the dining table, taller than Walker expected and younger, about forty, with a lean, tense, closely shaven face.

"Well, hello," Walker said, offering a hand to shake.

"Good evening," the man said, bowing instead of taking the offered hand. "I am Inoya."

He gestured at a chair and said, "Please be seated. I'm sorry I was late."

"Don't worry," Walker said, smiling, trying to sound friendly, feeling clumsy again. "I needed the sleep."

They talked while dining, the woman bringing each spare course: soup, veal, a salad, all prepared in Western style. The man himself seemed oddly Western; his English was slangy and easy, more American than British. He sometimes used his hands to emphasize a point. During one such exchange, Walker noticed that the last joint of his pinkie was missing, as if it had been chopped off. He thought at first that this must have been an accident in a machine shop, perhaps when the man was young; but while they talked and ate, the man never spoke in any detail about machine tools; he seemed to know almost nothing about them. He talked instead about sports, about New York, about politics, and Walker had to struggle against his uneasiness.

At last the dinner was over, and the man suggested they go into the game room for coffee. "Sure," Walker said. "Sounds good."

He followed the man to another room, with squashy leather chairs and a pool table and photographs of old prizefighters on the wall. Walker recognized Rocky Marciano and Muhammad Ali, and some other black American fighters; but most of the fighters were Japanese, men with tough flat faces and sharply cut sideburns. He didn't recognize any of them.

Inoya went to the bar and drew a cup of coffee from a large steel pot. He offered Walker a drink.

"No," Walker said, "coffee is fine."

The man brought him the cup and saucer and smiled in an odd way. "Some music, too," the man said, and then walked to the other side of the room. On shelves against the wall, there were modern tape decks, several VCRs, shelves of videotapes and CDs and phonograph records. But the man ignored them. He went instead to a machine that Walker knew was an old-fashioned wind-up Victorola. The man wound the machine, then lifted an old-fashioned 78 recording and placed it on the turntable. He laid the needle on the edge of the record.

"This is for you," he said softly.

The record began to play, with the worn sound of the old grooves coming through modern speakers, and Walker knew every word and every note. The singer was Jo Stafford and the song was "I'll Be Seeing You."

A vanished Japan started to flood through him, all the old familiar places . . . the small room at the end of the alley near the temple, the faces of people in the streets, averting their eyes at the sight of the conqueror, the loose clothes the women wore to hide their bodies, like baggy bloomers, their feet in white socks, jammed into wooden clogs, and the rubble everywhere. Walker sat down heavily in one of the leather chairs, while the song told of a small cafe, a park across the way, . . .

The man was standing above him now.

"This is for you, too," he said.

And handed Walker an old snapshot. And there he was, George Walker at twenty-two, in his Army uniform, with the woman beside him, holding the hand of the small boy. That lean and sweet and lovely woman. Tamayo. All three of them squinting into the sun, and the temple steps and some charred structures behind them.

Walker looked up at the man.

"You must be Kaz," he whispered.

"Yes . . ."

The song moved to its sad hopeful ending.

". . . and I'm going to kill you."

5

That was when Walker saw the gun, held loosely in the man's right
hand, with the chopped pinkie jutting out like a second barrel. The
man sat down on a stool beside the pool table, the gun in his hand,
staring at Walker for a long moment, as if hoping that Walker would
rise and try to fight. But Walker knew that he could not escape into
the night. Walker didn't even know where he was, didn't know
where to run, had seen behind this isolated house only trees and
woods under the stars. He could run, but would be hunted down in
terrain that the man he long ago nicknamed "Kaz" knew better than
Walker ever could.

The past crowded the room. He remembered stealing the phonograph from some Occupation warehouse of confiscated goods,
remembered buying the record "I'll Be Seeing You" in a PX, remembered playing it at night in the small room, the woman humming
the melody, saying the words, then singing with her sweet, tentative
voice, mimicking the English words and making them sound Japanese. He closed his eyes, hoping that when he opened them he would
be back in Cleveland, in his apartment or in the old shop, on some
evening before the letter arrived from Japan. But when he opened
them, seconds later, Kazuo was staring at him.

"I want to tell you a story," Kazuo said. "I've looked for you for
many years, to tell you the story. I could give you many details, but
most of them you know, don't you? Except the end, except the part
that happened after you left the theater."

He laid the gun flat on the pool table and then walked to the bar
for his cup of coffee, as if challenging Walker to go for the gun.
Walker didn't move.

"The story is about a woman with a child," Kazuo said. "And no husband. Her husband's name was Yoshimitsu, and he was a soldier in Manchuria when the Russians entered the war. Nobody knew if he was dead or alive, and the boy didn't even remember him. The boy only knew the war and the bombing and the hunger and remembered nothing before that. But all through the war, with all the fear, and the sound of the sirens, and the great fires, the boy never saw his mother cry."

"Please," Walker said. "Please don't . . ."

The man ignored him, sipped his coffee, speaking as if to himself.

"The war ended. The Americans came. There was still much hunger, but the bombs stopped, the fire stopped, the killing stopped, if not the dying. The woman met an American. And the American came to sleep with her. She wasn't unusual. Many women did the same. Their husbands were dead, their children were starving, they did what they had to do to survive. . . . Even my mother. But she didn't become a prostitute. She just met *you*."

Walker said, in a flat voice: "It was so long ago. Another lifetime, another country . . ."

"No, it was not so long ago," Kazuo said. "The woman did something far worse than merely survive, something much more foolish. She fell in love with the man. And he said he loved her."

"I *did*," Walker said. "I loved Tamayo."

"And the boy loved the American man too," Kazuo said. "He always remembered the chocolate the man brought when he came to the house near the burned temple in Asakusa. It was the great cliché of the Occupation, a country selling its emotions and loyalties and bodies for chocolate and cigarettes. But the boy liked the man, he learned English from the man, he trusted the man, he first played baseball with the man, when he came one Saturday with a bat and a ball and . . . this."

From the bar he tossed a worn leather baseball glove to Walker. It made a *phwock*ing sound when Walker caught it, and he remembered buying it in the same PX where he found the Jo Stafford, giving it to the boy, showing him how to dig a "pocket" in the glove, by slamming the ball over and over into the oiled glove, remembered Tamayo one night, by the light of a candle, showing him the boy, sound asleep with the glove and ball serving as a pillow. Long ago. In another country.

"But then the man had to go away, go home to his country across the sea," Kazuo said, laughing bitterly. "The boy was heartbroken. He had begun to call the man 'Daddy.' And suddenly 'Daddy' was leaving."

"Stop."

"And the man told the woman, who told the boy, that it was going to be all right. That was the best part. The American would go home, she told the boy, he would get some money and send it to the woman and she would get a ticket and go with the boy to America. They would get married. They would be happy. The man and the boy would go to the World Series. It sounded beautiful." He paused. "It was a fucking *lie.*"

The man slammed the top of the bar for emphasis, then came back to face Walker again.

"The woman waited and waited and waited," he said. "She played her phonograph record over and over; it was the only record she owned; and she waited for a letter that did not come. She would not eat. She could not sleep. She got sick, sick with her love for this man, sick from his cruelty, sick from his great lie, sick—"

Walker laid the glove on the floor and stood up. "It *wasn't* a lie. I loved her. I *loved* Tamayo. I never loved *any*one more than I loved her, not before, not after. But I . . ."

The emotion seeped out of him and his voice dribbled away.

"But you *what?*" Kazuo said acidly.

Walker sighed. He walked away from Kazuo to the bar, took a bottle of Scotch from a shelf, reached for a glass.

"Any ice?"

"In the covered bowl," Kazuo said.

Walker slipped two cubes in with the Scotch, swished them around, the cubes making a clunking sound against the thick glass.

His hands were shaking but he took a long sip, then stared at the inside of the glass.

"I was a boy then," he said.

"So was I."

"But your mother was a *woman*."

"She was twenty-four the year you left."

Walker looked at him in disbelief. "No . . . She seemed . . ."

"The war made everybody seem older."

Walker said nothing; he knew this was true. He drained the glass, then splashed more scotch on top of the ice. His hands shook. He wished he had a cigarette.

"How old was she when—"

"Twenty-seven."

Walker turned his back on Kazuo and made a choking sound, and breathed in deeply, and then his large soft body began to heave. The only sound was his dry, wracking sobs. When he turned around again, Kazuo had the gun in his hand. Walker looked lost and forlorn.

"Go ahead," Walker said in a flat voice. "Do it. I'm sick of this fucking life business."

6

Kazuo stared at him. And Walker saw the man's eyes well up with emotion. Walker thought: he's going to kill me and I don't care.

"Look, maybe it doesn't matter now, but I did want you to come to America," he said. "I started writing a letter five or six times . . ." He paused. "But when I went home, there were no jobs. I had no money. I was living at home with my parents and my sisters, I didn't know how to explain that . . ."

"That you were bringing home two *Japs*?"

"No, no, that wasn't it. I didn't know how to explain to *Tamayo* that I wasn't *rich*, that I had nothing, that I had no home for her or you, that America wasn't the land of milk and honey. I couldn't explain that I didn't even have the money for the airplane tickets. I was ashamed of myself. Weeks went by, and then months, and then I couldn't explain to her why I hadn't written and . . ."

He shook his head.

"I'm sorry. I'm so goddamned sorry."

Kazuo stood there, lost in thought, his body limp now, the gun hand hanging down. They said nothing to each other for a long moment and then both were aware of the sound of the phonograph needle, stuck in the last soundless groove. Kazuo blinked, then walked over, lifted the needle off the record and put down the gun. He lifted the record off the turntable and then abruptly, violently broke it in half. He dropped the pieces on the floor, then picked up the gun again. He stared at the broken pieces of the record.

"Finish your drink," he whispered.

Walker stared at him, then sipped the Scotch and placed the glass on the bar. He turned, prepared to die. Kazuo raised the gun once more, his face a tight grid, and pointed it at Walker's head. The older man could feel his heart pounding.

"Pack your bag and get out of here, you son of a bitch."

He lowered his extended arm, slipped the gun into his jacket pocket and looked off toward the photographs of the prizefighters. He picked up his coffee cup and saucer and made a face as he sipped the cold brew.

Walker said in a hoarse voice, "I wish we'd all had a different life."

"Shut up," Kazuo said. " Go."

Walker started from the bar but could feel nothing in his legs. I'm not drunk, he thought, it can't be the drink. Kazuo wouldn't look at him. But then Walker paused at the pool table, steadied himself with a hand.

"What about you, Kaz?" he said softly. "What did *you* do?"

The younger man turned and stared at Walker, his eyes full of hurt and old anger, his hard face laced with little rivers of emotion. He held the coffee cup with the chopped finger extended, almost daintily.

"I survived," he said. "I survived."

After the War

1

When Akio arrived home at last, he felt as if exhaustion had eroded his bones. He'd sent his assistants a fax from Paris, saying that he could get home on his own, he didn't need a car, everything could wait for the following day. Now he was sorry they weren't at the baggage area to meet him; he was forced to find a porter to carry the camera cases to the taxi; he had to exchange a jumble of francs and marks for yen, just to tip the porter and pay the taxi. He dozed all the way from Narita to the apartment in Shinjuku, with the images of two long months moving in and out of focus in his mind: men hammering at the Berlin Wall and snipers shooting in Bucharest and that great joyous throng roaring in Prague as Havel came to the balcony in triumph. He saw the faces of old men weeping, young girls waving flags, and everywhere, people smiling in joy. He had photographed them all. But they seemed to remain there in his mind as a blur, still demanding to be given form and life. He wished all of them would go away.

At the apartment house, the old super found a small cart for the camera cases and gave Akio a carton of old mail. Inside the door, he laid the cases on the floor, ignored the mail and went straight to the bedroom. He undressed in slow motion and then fell on the bed, limp and empty. These nine weeks had been too much of everything. Too many crowds. Too much exuberance. Too many hotels. Too much bad food riddled with suet and gristle. And now, choked with jet lag, eaten by loneliness, he fell into a deep, dreamless sleep.

Eleven hours later, he came awake. He shaved, showered and

dressed and then went to the kitchen and quietly made tea. He ignored the television and could not switch on the radio; he was sick of news, sick of its urgency. He smoked a cigarette and gazed out at the cold afternoon light. Then he started going through the mail. He made separate piles for bills, for magazines, for advertising circulars. There was a card from his friend Noriyuki, who was covering the war in El Salvador, and a letter from his sister in San Francisco, who was having problems with her middle son. Then he saw the envelope from the Hilltop Hotel. His name and address were written in English. And he would know the bold handwriting anywhere.

Diane.

He held the envelope for a long moment and then sat back and lit another cigarette.

Diane. Here. In Tokyo. At the Hilltop Hotel in Jimbocho.

He opened the envelope slowly and then read the note on the hotel stationery.

Akio, it said. *I'll be in Tokyo for ten days, working on a story. I'd love to see you. Best, Diane*

That was all. Blunt and direct. As always.

He looked at the date on the envelope, and then at the calendar on his wristwatch. She would be here for two more days. Two days. He tried to remember how long it had been since he'd seen her. Five years? Six? Yes, it was six years since he'd packed his bags and left her behind in New York, never to return. And then he realized that it was fifteen years since he'd met her, fifteen years since the fall of Saigon, with all of them running in the streets of Cholon, the sound of artillery rumbling in the distance and rumors filling the air. The ARVN were stripping off their uniforms and the Americans were desperate to get to the embassy. All of them except Diane. She was a kid then, a good reporter, crazy brave with the craziness of the young.

"You have to go," he told her. "You can't stay."

"I want to see it," she said. "I want to see the end of it."

"These are kid soldiers," he said. "Farmers from the north. Led by tough old veterans. When they get here, they won't care if you're a reporter or not. You're a Westerner. Worse, an American. Their job is killing people like you."

"I'll take that chance."

That night they stayed together in a room on a high floor of the Caravel. They could see the distant explosions of artillery, the sky suddenly bright, then dark again. They could hear airplanes and helicopters. Somewhere nearby, machine guns were hammering. It was oddly beautiful. They made furious love. In the morning the war was over. He drove her through the panicky streets and forced her, sobbing and angry, over the wall into the compound of the American Embassy. She left on the next-to-last helicopter, ahead of the ambassador and his dog.

She shouted, "I'll see you in Tokyo."

She'd kept her word.

And that was simply the beginning.

Fifteen years . . .

He picked up the telephone.

2

She looked more beautiful than ever in the dim light of the restaurant and that made it worse. She had an oval face and a frank, wide mouth and green eyes spaced widely apart. The mole on her left cheek only emphasized the perfection of her face. Her beauty had helped her as a reporter, of course, but it had also been her curse. The older reporters, the tough old editors, simply couldn't believe that someone that beautiful could also be a serious reporter. To overcome the beauty, she'd been forced to work harder than most of the others. Once, when they lived together in New York, she told Akio that she couldn't wait until she got older and looked worse; but she *was* looking forward to that day. "Then they'll take me seriously at last," she said, and laughed. Across the table from her now, he thought she looked more beautiful than ever. And remembered that he'd always taken her seriously. Too damned seriously.

"Tokyo has changed so much," she said. "It's so . . . *fat*."

"The correct word is *expensive*," he said, in his flawless English, the slang and rhythms perfected in American wars and in American beds.

"I had a crew covering the department stores," she said. "And I spent two months' pay just doing the story."

"You used to say that you'd never do television," Akio said.

"I was young," she said, and smiled. "You once swore to me, if I recall, that you'd never do fashion."

"I gave that up three years ago," he said.

"I know," she said. "I read it in some gossip column and I was happy for you."

There was an awkward moment, as if she didn't know what to say next.

"Thank you," he said, in a formal way. "For caring about me, if that's the word."

She poked a spoon through her coffee, as if searching for words that would say as little as possible.

"Reporting . . . the wars . . . the streets . . . that's really your life," she said.

"Yes," he said, and smiled. "That's my life. Being sent places to be pushed around by the police."

She laughed.

"It was your life too," he added. "And you were very good at it. Better than almost anyone I ever met." He glanced away, at the other diners, at a waiter. He motioned for more coffee.

"I loved reporting," she said.

"You can still do it."

She shifted again. "Tell me about Europe," she said.

He did. She listened. Her face began to change, her eyes growing moist. She still had that totally focused quality of making him feel that, in that moment, there were no other human beings on the earth. He loved that quality once. Now it made him uncomfortable, too open, naked, *defenseless*. For the first time that evening, he thought that calling her might have been a mistake.

"You'd have loved Eastern Europe," he said, trying to be polite. "It's the greatest story since Vietnam."

"I wish I'd been there too."

"It isn't over. Go now."

"I can't," she said. "They—"

She shrugged and broke off, and then struggled back to focus. She tried to explain to Akio what it meant to be an anchorwoman, sitting each day in a studio, reading the news off a TelePrompTer. She talked about how parochial the Americans were; if the story didn't involve Americans or threaten them, they turned off. That's why they didn't care much about Eastern Europe.

"Besides, there aren't enough bodies," she said. "They want dead people and Eastern Europe doesn't have enough of them. You remember how it was in Vietnam: send more bang-bang. So they've sent me here."

"There are no bodies here either," Akio said. "And no bang-bang at all."

"No, but there's a lot of money. They *are* interested in money."

He laughed, but remembered the way she fought him in the swollen crowd of Vietnamese, pushing him off, demanding to stay, her hair wild and her eyes furious as he shoved her up and over the fence. There were plenty of bodies in that story.

"You should go to Eastern Europe anyway," he said. "If you don't, you'll miss the twentieth century."

"I miss you more."

"Please don't say things like that," he said. "I'm too old for that game."

"It's not a game," she said.

"Yes, it is," he said. "Or *was*. But you played by one set of rules and I was playing by another."

There was a long moment of silence. They could hear the other diners, cups touching saucers, fragments of words, a burst of laughter.

"Akio, please," she said, her voice low. "The one thing I didn't want to do when I came here is make you feel bitter again." She turned away, her eyes moving around the restaurant. "So, goddamnit, for what it's worth, I'm sorry I said I missed you. Okay? Even though I have missed you. And do. And for a long, long time."

He said nothing then and called for the check and paid with a credit card.

At the door, he murmured: "I missed you too."

3

They walked back to the hotel through the deserted streets of Kanda. The night was cool. He did not take her hand. She said that she loved this area, the bookstores and the shops that sold paper and the tiny restaurants and the sense of an older Tokyo. He pointed at the signs of the ski shops and sporting goods stores, marching on the district, eating the bookstores.

"It's the money now," he said. "Money runs everything. The cost of land is so high, there's no room anymore for a man who sells books."

"Like New York," she said.

"Worse," he said. He gestured at the avenue. "You ought to bring your crew down here. It's a good story. Not as sexy as the car business but it is about money."

She didn't say anything for a while; she clearly didn't want to talk about stories for television. They stood awkwardly on a corner. Akio lit a cigarette as Diane looked up the avenue toward the hotel. She seemed to tremble, then cleared her throat, started to talk again.

"I remember the time we—"

"Don't," he said. "That's all behind us, Diane. Gone. Dead."

But in his mind, he saw them on this same corner, long ago, holding hands in a warm Tokyo summer rain, soaked to the skin, their shoes ruined, walking up the long hill to the hotel. The war was over. The killing and the dying had ended. Men and women could love each other without worrying about dying tomorrow. He remembered that: the rain of Tokyo. Falling and falling, a constant, a texture, healing the injured world. They'd stayed in the room for forty-eight hours. They made vows. They spoke about a future. They laughed. They ate. They made love. Far from the place where bodies were covered by flies in the rice paddies. Far from the thumping sound of helicopters. Miles from the bang-bang. Here in gray, rainy Tokyo. After Vietnam.

Now he felt unable to move. He stood on the corner, hands in his pockets, a few feet from this woman he once loved more than anyone on earth. He couldn't make small talk. But he needed to know something else. And didn't know how to begin. This wasn't an interview. There was no script. And he thought: Just begin. Just go straight at it.

"How's your husband?" Akio said.

"Gone."

He looked at her.

"I thought he—you told me once that he was good for you."

"He was," she said. "But I was bad for him."

She didn't look at him. A slight wind rose. Some banners flapped above the closed shops.

"He brought me to television, all right, but I became the star, not him," she said. "He couldn't handle that. Not many men can. But it sure did bring out the asshole in him. He lost one job, got another, lost that, and of course, he blamed me. They started calling him by my name. It ruined him. He started drinking, chasing models who were a foot taller than he was. That's where he started with the cocaine. The girls think it keeps them thin." She laughed. "Then one night, a couple of years ago, he asked me for ten thousand dollars. I gave it to him and he packed up and left."

"He was a nice boy," Akio lied, remembering the time he met the man in New York, with his fresh face and hot, ambitious eyes. He remembered feeling danger, a vague threat, as the man hovered around Diane at the cocktail party, telling her he was a producer and she should be in television. Telling her she was beautiful and intelligent and serious. Telling her she was a sure thing.

"No," she said, as a taxi hurried by and the Tokyo air turned damp. "He was a boy, all right. But he wasn't nice."

"Neither were you."

"No. Neither was I."

Then he remembered coming back to New York from Nicaragua after three weeks away, dozing in the taxi from Kennedy, and going to their apartment to find her gone, along with her clothes and cosmetics, her towels and her teapot. Her books had been pulled from the bookcase, leaving spaces like missing teeth. There was a note that time too. As always, it was blunt and direct. The next day, he'd called a friend to find her new telephone number. He talked to her carefully at first, caging his emotions. But he couldn't sustain the act. He didn't want an accounting from her; he set aside his pride and pleaded with her to come back. She refused. She was sorry, she said, but she had to make this decision on her own, this was serious, more serious than anything in her life. She'd found this man, she said, or he'd found her, or maybe they just found each other, and she was going to change her life. She was rising to a new level. To television. It wasn't very serious, but it was a move up. Yes, he said, like the escape over the wall into the embassy. She said she had hoped he wouldn't be so bitter.

"Maybe I'm making a mistake," she said. "But I won't know until I try."

That was it. Abrupt and forceful. His Diane. And when he hung up the phone, he understood that he couldn't live in New York anymore, knowing that she was out there in the same city with this new man, this worthless boy with the hot and greedy eyes. That night he went home to pack. And had not seen her again until now.

"But you know," she said, standing in a Tokyo street, on this chilly night, years later, "I paid for that mistake. I paid for not being nice. I lost you."

A chilly rain began to fall, frail at first, and then in great spattering drops. He took her hand. Then led her across the street, starting up the hill as they had done one reckless night a lifetime ago. At first she was annoyed with the rain, shielding her hair with her jacket, wobbling on her high heels. And then, as if remembering that old night, she started to laugh. She kicked off her shoes. She grabbed Akio and hugged him and then moved up the hill with him, through the drowned world.

"I came here to get you," she said.

"All right," he said. "You've got me."

The Opponent

1

The Kid lay alone in the dressing room, stretched out on his back on a rubbing table. He wasn't really a kid anymore. He was thirty-one years old, and as the sportswriters would say, his future was behind him. But here he was again, doing the job he'd done as a boy. His eyes wandered and he saw his robe on a hanger. Some of the sequins had come unraveled, but he remembered first wearing the robe for that fight in Puerto Rico, when he was a champion and nobody could touch him and the punches came in blazing flurries and they were talking about him as one of the greatest fighters in the history of the lightweight division. A long time ago.

Now he was in Tokyo. He could still make 135, but he wasn't a champion anymore; he was just an opponent, a Name brought in for a payday. He was fighting some Japanese puncher, one of those wild-swinging young men who rise and fall very quickly, the kind of fighter The Kid once used for target practice. He remembered a night when he was coming up and fought one of these bangers at the Felt Forum in Madison Square Garden. The banger came in a free-swinging rush, all muscle and fury, and The Kid speared him with the jab, mystified him with combinations, cut him over both eyes, whirled, danced, moved, even did the boogaloo; and when the big bad banger was exhausted and bleeding, The Kid stepped in, faked a hook, and dropped a perfect right hand on the guy's chin. They could have counted a hundred. And the next day, the sports-writers said that The Kid was going to be one of the great ones. Yeah. True. The story was in the scrapbooks, back home in Miami.

The Kid's reverie was broken by the roar of the crowd outside. He'd heard that roar in many places. Sometimes they'd even roared for The Kid. Here the roar was brief, even polite. Everybody was polite here. Even the sportswriters were polite and that was definitely something new for The Kid. Hell, they even called him mister. Mr. Kid. Or Kid-*san*. And bowed in respect. When they did that, The Kid had to work hard to keep from laughing. Not at them. Hell, no. They were nice. He wanted to laugh at the whole lousy shithouse of a racket where he'd spent his life. In boxing, no matter where you went in the world, nobody was ever polite. Not even to champions.

The door opened. Charlie Johnson walked in, followed by a Japanese man. Ozaki. The promoter. The sound from the arena was briefly louder and then they closed the door. Johnson was the booker. The Kid didn't have a manager anymore, just a booker, who found him fights wherever he could get them. He'd booked The Kid into a lot of strange places in the years since he lost the title. Bangkok. Manila. Even once in Africa. Television was really something. Made you famous all over the fucking world. Made you money, too. As long as you kept winning. When you stopped winning, when you lost two fights, then drew another, then won a decision, then lost two more, hey, you were still famous, but you became an opponent. You were the respectable Name who was sent places to get beat by the new kid who was coming up. That's what The Kid was now. An opponent. A good Name to be listed in some other guy's record. When he was coming up, The Kid beat a few guys like that himself.

"How you feelin', Kid?" Charlie Johnson said.

"Pretty good," The Kid said.

"Get over the jet lag?"

"I guess. I never really get over it, you know."

Charlie Johnson laughed.

"You get as old as me, Kid, you feel happy just gettin' up and not pissin' blood."

The Kid smiled.

"How long now?" he said.

"Twenty minutes," Johnson said, glancing at his watch. He turned to Ozaki. The promoter was short and thick-necked and had a scar on his left cheekbone. "Right? Maybe twenty minutes?"

"Yes," the promoter said. "Twenty minutes, maybe less." There was another polite roar outside in the arena. Ozaki smiled in a mirthless way, moving his head toward the noise beyond the door. "Maybe much faster."

The Kid sat up and started taping his hands. Since his days in the amateurs, he had always taped his own hands. Some fighters had the seconds do it. But The Kid liked the feeling of molding his hand into something that was solid and hard but still flexible. When he boxed, he always kept his hands loose. Amateurs fought with their fists clenched and tired their arms.

"The guy I'm fightin'," The Kid said, "can he fight any?"

"He's a banger," Charlie Johnson said. He glanced at the promoter again, but said nothing.

"Twenty-seven fights," the promoter said. "Twenty-seven knock-outs."

Ozaki said this as if even he didn't believe it.

"The last three fights," Johnson said, "he sold the joint out."

The promoter said, "And if he beats you, he will fight for championship."

"*If* he beats me," The Kid said, and smiled.

"He *must* win," Ozaki said.

The sentence hung in the air like a command. The Kid looked at Charlie Johnson but the booker was staring at an old fight poster on the wall.

"I see," The Kid said, thinking: it's like a movie, some old turkey about racket guys and fighters. Jesus.

Johnson took the promoter to the door and whispered something as the man went out. Then he turned to face The Kid.

"Don't take the guy serious," Johnson said. "He seen too many fuckin' movies."

"So did I," The Kid said.

He got up now and threw some punches at the air and then the door opened again and three more Japanese men came in. "These are your cornermen," Johnson explained. The Kid nodded. At this stage of his career the promoters never paid for cornermen to fly from the States. He picked up local guys, paid them as little as possible, and hoped for the best. All he really needed was a cut man who didn't blind him. The three men bowed. They were dressed identically in slacks and white sweaters. There were no names on the sweaters. The smallest man explained with gestures that he would handle the cuts for Mr. Kid and then they were gone. The Kid sat down again.

"How long now, Charlie?" The Kid said, and yawned.

"We better go."

2

As he waited in his corner, rubbing the thin soles of his old boxing shoes in resin, listening to announcements that he could not understand, The Kid gazed out at the audience. There were groups of Japanese men dressed like movie gangsters, with striped suits and dark glasses. There were young people dressed like punks, with shaved skulls or hair dyed purple or pink. Everybody smoked cigarettes. He saw only a few women, including one blonde who looked as if she'd walked into the wrong building. He remembered coming out of dressing rooms years ago and seeing guys he'd grown up with, guys from the army, guys from the gym, and girls: oh, yeah, girls, with hot eyes and hotter bodies. A lot of them were blondes, even some of the black chicks. But now he was in a place where he knew absolutely nobody. He didn't even know the names of the cornermen. Oh well: fuck it. Just do the job. Pick up the ten Gs. Give Johnson his piece. Go home. He saw Johnson sitting in the first row behind the press, with Ozaki beside him. Both men looked nervous. A nicotine fog hung over the arena.

He glanced at the young man he was fighting. He had a flat face with wide-spaced eyes and a square-backed haircut. His shoulders were broad. He looked bigger than 135 pounds and The Kid knew that he probably was. You always took that chance when you fought in places where the other guy controlled the scales. Win or lose, The Kid thought, I gotta be the best lightweight in the welterweight division. Then a grave little guy in a tuxedo started announcing the main event. He heard his own name and walked to the center of the ring, the frayed sequin robe loose on his shoulders. There was some scattered, polite applause. Then they announced the other guy. Hanada. From Osaka. Cheers and shouts. They were very polite here, but in a boxing arena the crowd almost always loses its manners, sooner or later. The Kid smiled.

He listened as the referee gave the instructions in Japanese. Hanada was staring at him, and The Kid looked up, saw the burning eyes and flaring nostrils, saw Hanada doing his impression of Roberto Duran, and smiled again. Not because the guy was nothing. But because The Kid used to pull this act himself, long ago, when he was young and thought he was unbeatable. His smile seemed to push Hanada's anger to a level beyond the usual ferocious pose. The Japanese fighter snorted. He bared his teeth. He slapped The Kid's gloves hard at the end of the instructions and there were cheers from the Osaka gangsters down front. Oh well, The Kid thought: he'll learn.

The Kid walked back to his corner and one of the seconds took his robe and jammed in the mouthpiece, and there was the bell. Hanada came on a run, launching a big swinging right hand, and The Kid stepped to the side and let him go by. Hanada slammed into the ropes, turned, snarled, and came at him again. The Kid popped a jab, then another, not punches really, but taps, to keep Hanada away. That wasn't easy. Hanada came in a snorting rush again, slamming into The Kid, and started hammering at the body. The Kid thought: okay, he can bang, but he's not a puncher. Too sloppy, the punches too wide. The Kid tied him up.

The referee broke the clinch, and The Kid danced to his own

right, away from Hanada's right hand. Then Hanada came again, the right hand cocked, and The Kid bent at the knees and hit him with a hook as he came in. Hanada wobbled. The Kid went at him, threw a combination, all speed and sass, and then stepped briskly away to safety. He saw confusion in Hanada's face now and his cornermen shouting instructions. All right, The Kid thought: that'll keep him from getting *too* fucking fresh.

The rest of the round went that way: Hanada rushing, The Kid popping him and moving away. And then he heard the bell. On his stool, The Kid took deep breaths. For ten grand, he thought, I'll give them a fucking show. He went out and gave them a show in the second round and the third, dancing, moving, avoiding the clumsy rushes of the young man from Osaka. He didn't look at Johnson or the Japanese promoter. He tried to stay loose and calm and empty. Not completely empty. Between rounds, he saw Miami, a flicker of palm trees. His woman, Maria. Her round ass. Her luscious breasts. He thought about going home with $10,000 dollars. And went out for the fourth round.

A minute into the round, Hanada hit him under the heart with a right hand and The Kid went numb. He grabbed, he held, he clinched. But he could't feel anything on the left side of his body and his arm was dead. When he looked at Hanada, the young man's eyes had a hard, blank, remorseless look, and he was coming in, his mouth tight, and The Kid waited, tried to time the hook, to step inside the arc of Hanada's swinging right hand. He saw the freight train coming, unloaded his own right, and hit Hanada on the chin. The young man from Osaka went down.

The place exploded in noise, and The Kid went to the neutral corner, as Hanada flopped over on the canvas, head down, and grabbed for the lower strand of the ropes. *Don't get up,* The Kid thought. *Please don't get up, please, stay there, don't get up, I'm old and I'm shot, and I'm still numb from your fuckin' right hand. Stay there. Don't get up.*

But Hanada was up at eight, suddenly very young, looking at his frantic corner, where a second was motioning with a left hand, poking it straight out, telling him to jab, and the referee was looking at him, and then Hanada was coming again. He didn't bother with the jab. He was furious and ashamed, and he came right at The Kid. There was no elegance in him, no style. Just fury and anger. The Kid jabbed with the dead arm and Hanada walked through the jab and hit him a glancing punch alongside the head with the right hand and then drove a hook into The Kid's belly. The Kid's right leg rose in shock and he tried to hold but Hanada shoved him and threw a wild right hand that missed, and another hook to the ribs, and The Kid felt as if his shoes were filled with water. He tried to move to the right, but couldn't do it. He didn't see the last punch. But the world went suddenly white. He heard a high piercing sound. A billion tiny blue dots appeared. And he felt a sudden blank exhausted peace.

3

In the dressing room, he lay in silence for a long time. Two of the cornermen were there, but they spoke no English. On the ceiling, The Kid saw a stain that looked like Florida. He would have to call Maria. She always worried. He would tell her that he had fought. That he'd knocked the guy down. That he'd been knocked out. She would cry. In some odd way, that made him feel good. His first wife never cried. She only got mad.

Johnson came in with the promoter.

"Nice fight," Johnson said. "But we got a problem."

"What do you mean, a problem?"

"Ozaki-*san* here, he doesn't want to pay you," Johnson said. "Because you knocked his guy down."

"Are you bullshittin' me?" The Kid said.

He turned and got up, glancing at a mirror over the sink, and for the first time realized that his left eye was almost shut. Color of an eggplant. That last punch must have done it.

"He says you embarrassed his guy by knockin' him down."

"I get paid to knock people down," The Kid said.

"Well, Kid, you see—"

Johnson looked away, trying to form words.

"You promised him a *tank* job?" The Kid said. "You told him I'd go in the fuckin' *water*?"

"Well, not exactly . . ."

The promoter intervened. "We had deal," Ozaki growled, in a Japanese version of the movie tough guy manner. "You suppose to lose. It was part of—"

"Get out of here," The Kid whispered. "*Both* of you. Get the fuck out of here."

Then the door opened again and Hanada stood there, in jeans and a Hawaiian shirt. A few other men were behind him. One of them was in a suit. He was the translator. Hanada paused, then smiled and stepped into the dressing room. Ozaki looked uneasy.

"Kid-*san*," the translator said. "Hanada wants to thank you for the very good fight."

Hanada bowed, then embraced The Kid. He said something in Japanese, then bowed again.

"He wants to tell you it was the best fight of his life," the translator said. "He says he saw you on television when he was boy in Osaka. He says it was big honor to fight you."

"Thanks," The Kid said. "Tell him he's a terrific puncher. Tell him I think he's got a ton of heart. A lot of guys, they wouldn't'a got up after takin' the shot I hit him."

The translator told Hanada what The Kid said, and the Japanese fighter bowed. Johnson and the promoter waited on the side, whispering. Hanada spoke again.

"He says that if he wins the championship," the translator said, "he would be happy to fight you again."

"No," The Kid said. "That's it. I'm packin' it in. I'm retired."

Johnson heard this. "Well, that's not exactly true. The Kid's just depressed after a hard fight. We got a very good offer from Manila, and maybe a rematch here—"

"Shut up, Charlie," The Kid said. "I'm finished with you too. I'm finished with all this shit."

Johnson backed up and then slipped out the door. Ozaki watched him go, glanced at his watch. The translator was whispering to Hanada. The young fighter looked embarrassed.

"You know why I'm packin' it in?" The Kid said to Hanada. "This bum over here—" He pointed at Ozaki. "He doesn't want to pay me my full purse. He says I embarrassed him by knockin' you down. Imagine that? Well, it's been too fuckin' long now I had to deal with pricks like this. And you know something else, Hanada? Something *more* important? You stay in this racket as long as me, you'll have to deal with these shitbags too."

When the translator finished explaining this, Hanada exploded. He shouted at Ozaki in Japanese, slamming the rubbing table with an open hand. Color drained from the promoter's face. Then Hanada put an arm around The Kid. He was shouting now, addressing the room, full of anger and a kind of shame.

"He says you are brothers," the translator explained to The Kid. "He says if you are not paid, he will retire too."

"Tell him I think he's nuts," The Kid said, "but okay, if he says so, we're brothers."

Ozaki's eyes glittered, his mouth tightened to a slit. He started for the door, but Hanada blocked his way, still snarling at him in guttural Japanese. The door opened from outside. Two men in gangster suits stood there. The Kid walked over and said: "Get the fuck out of here." He kicked the door shut and locked it. Then he and Hanada turned together to the promoter.

"You want to walk out of here, I'll take it now," The Kid said. "The whole ten grand. In cash."

Ozaki was still for a long moment, then backed up a few steps, his eyes widening and closing, closing and widening. He took out a pack of Marlboro Lights, forcing a reasonable smile to spread on his face like a stain. He lit up in a deliberate way without looking at the two fighters. He inhaled deeply. Then as smoke leaked from his mouth, he took a checkbook from his jacket pocket. He signed a check, the cigarette burning between two fingers of his writing hand. He walked to the door, unlocked it, opened it a crack, with Hanada as close to him as an arresting officer, and handed the check to one of the young men in gangster suits. The young man hurried off to get the cash. The Kid glimpsed Johnson waiting alone in the corridor but closed the door without a word to him. They were all still for a moment. Ozaki stared at an old fight poster and smoked in a jittery way. Finally, Hanada smiled and said something in Japanese.

"Now," the translator explained, "you must please get dressed. And then Hanada-*san* will be honored to buy you dinner."

"All right, brother," The Kid said to Hanada. "But tonight, the honor is mine."

The 48th Ronin

1

Jenkins hated the mornings now. Once the morning was the best time of his day, and he rose with the sounds of dawn in the apartment on the top floor of the building in Kichijoji. From his window on the third floor, he could see for miles. There were farms here then, and tall trees undamaged by the war and rice paddies turned a glossy red by the sun. He would hear cocks crowing and the sound of a distant radio and the barking of a few lonesome dogs. He would make tea and then go to the balcony and sip the tea and listen to the shuffling sound of wooden sandals and the blurred voices of women and then inhale the odors of the Japanese morning.

That was 1951. That year, Jenkins was twenty-seven years old.

Now, in the crowded apartment, he sat alone and was often afraid. He was the last tenant left in the building and when he gazed out from his balcony now he no longer saw wash drying on clotheslines or futon mats being aired on the rooftops. He no longer saw men leaving for work on bicycles or women in kimonos, their socks, called *tabi*, a dazzling white, heading for the old market. The market was gone, replaced by a shopping center, and there was a gigantic department store where there once were open fields. He passed restaurants where slick young men charmed sleek young women and drove away in fancy cars; Jenkins could remember when they were shops that sold traps for the many rats.

But the great change was not what made him afraid. It was the young man, Suzuki Junior, who came to Jenkins' door at least once a week now, always by surprise. At first, the young man's voice was irritated. He wanted the old *gaijin* to move, for he wanted to tear down the old building and erect some great and gleaming tower. Jenkins mumbled and smiled and evaded the young man's urgings. But now when the young man came, he was threatening. He presented Jenkins with legal forms. He demanded fingerprint records. He spoke about the police. And if the police didn't do the job, the young man said, then something worse might happen.

"Your father wouldn't say such things," Jenkins said one morning, in his American-accented Japanese.

"My father is dead," the young man said, and walked away.

Yes, Jenkins thought. *I know.* Suzuki-*san*, with whom he would drink tea at the end of day and speak about literature: dead. He had been the owner of the building but was never some cartoon of a landlord. When they first met, in 1951, the wars were all over (no matter what they were doing to each other in Korea), and Suzuki-*san* was happy with life. Now he was gone, and he had not been the first of the old crowd to die. Mr. Yamamoto from the first floor, lover of baseball, quick with jokes: he died in '63, still sick with malaria from the Philippines. Mr. Fukuzawa from the second floor, fat, creator of great feasts, father of three fat daughters, married to a sweet fat woman: he died in '69, seated before a bowl of *soba*, happy right to the end. Dead too was the old woman Jenkins first saw when both were young. She was shining shoes alongside the men at the train station, near the black market, and she was always laughing, not imprisoned in silence like the old soldiers whose pride was wounded by shining the shoes of other men. She saved her money, opened a small restaurant, married a construction worker, had three children, grew old, outlived her husband, and died alone.

They'd all lived in that building, in the years after Jenkins returned from New York. He first saw Tokyo in October of 1945 and fell to the rubbled earth and wept. He stayed on with the army of the Occupation, intoxicated by the culture of these people who had so recently been his enemy. He learned some crude Japanese, fell in love several times, bought too many books, and returned to the

States after discharge, vowing to return. He enrolled at Columbia on the GI Bill and took a degree in Japanese studies. The more he read and learned, the more the distant country blossomed in his imagination; the more he saw of his own country, the more he wanted to return to the other. He worked at two jobs and saved his money. The plan was always the same: to return to Japan and live there for the rest of his days.

The plan was fulfilled, although he soon learned that life was never as simple as any plan conceived in a furnished room in New York. When Jenkins first arrived, there was a pale lovely woman named Murasaki living alone in a single six-tatami-mat room. Jenkins loved her madly and called her Lady Murasaki after the author of *The Tale of Genji*. Unlike the others in his building, she didn't die, but she didn't love him back. She had loved a sweet boy who died on Okinawa in the war and insisted that she could never love another man. When Jenkins told her, with great passion, that love was always possible (for he was young too), she began to sob and the next day she was gone. Looking back years later, writing about her in his journal, Jenkins realized that her departure was a kind of death too.

2

There had been other women, of course, and a wife too. But few understood his romantic vision of Japan, and even the wife had left him after a year. Now he was alone with the gatherings and accumulations of his life. Most of them were books.

In the early years in the apartment in Kichijoji, his books filled the shelves on one wall. He worked as an interpreter then, because there were so few Japanese who knew English and almost no Americans who knew Japanese. For a long time, American companies were everywhere in Japan and Jenkins sat with visiting businessmen in restaurants and in geisha houses, trying clumsily to translate witticisms, failing to translate puns, trying anxiously to keep up with the flow of information about facts and figures that bored him into numbness. In the early sixties, after the end of the Occupation, after the Olympic Games, the American companies were slowly replaced by the revived Japanese corporations, more young people learned English, and Jenkins stopped interpreting and became a translator. This was a great relief. He didn't have to supply the correct word instantly, didn't have to anticipate the next, didn't have to convert himself into a mere instrument. He could ponder, judge, choose; he could consult his many dictionaries; he could seek the advice of others. An interpreter was a kind of performer; a translator was really a scholar. He translated reports, articles, an occasional academic piece, and although the money was never very good, it was more than enough to pay for his life in the apartment in Kichijoji. It even encouraged him to marry that time.

"You love your books more than you love me," his wife had said to him one night. And he thought about this, and the way the books now filled shelves on all the walls, and he said to her, sadly and with a certain remorse, "That's true."

She was twenty-five years old and very thin and believed that if she left him, her prospects would not be good. But no woman could live with such a man. That night she went to speak to him about her hurt, but he was absorbed in one of his books. She went off soon after that and told him by letter that she wanted a divorce and, of course, he consented. "I think I simply can't be married," he wrote to his sister in California. "I'm too strange. I thought I could be a decent husband. But now I might never know." His ex-wife discovered that her prospects were better than she thought; she sent him a card when she married again and then after the birth of each of her three children. But he had not heard from her now in fifteen years.

No matter. In the apartment, he had constructed his own world, the Japan that Jenkins had invented for himself in New York, the Japan he believed was immortal, the Japan that had drawn him into permanent exile from his own country. There were woodcuts by Hokusai and Hiroshige and Utamaro. There were stacked record-

ings of *gagaku* music, all flutes and drums and bronze bells, as slow
as the twelfth century. A sixteenth-century *nihonto* sword dangled
from a peg on the side of one of the bookcases. Over the doorway, a
small collection of *Noh* masks glowered at Jenkins and his few visitors. He had even mastered the tea ceremony. In these rooms, Jenkins read the histories and legends, enchanted by the stoic nobility of
failure in so many Japanese tales, identifying more with the trag-
edies of the nation's long history than its extraordinary achieve-
ments. Suzuki-*san* even laughed at this once: "You are the American
ronin. You love failure. You hope to be a martyr."

Jenkins didn't think of himself as a failure, nor did he see himself
as a *ronin*, one of the forty-seven legendary eighteenth century
samurai who killed themselves after avenging the death of their
lord. They might have been martyrs; they were not failures. They
lived and died according to the samurai code of *bushido* and so succeeded in full completion of their lives; Jenkins had no such code.
When the forty-seven *ronin* had avenged their lord and committed
suicide according to the code, they were buried with their master in
the Sengakuji temple; Jenkins knew he would be buried alone in a
place he did not know and could not imagine. He was, he wrote
sadly in his journal, more of a curator of things past than a recorder
of the present or prophet of the future. In his bookcases (which now
filled what had been open space in the second room, with shelves in
aisles like a library) he had preserved the Japan that young men like
Suzuki Junior did not know or did not honor. The young Japanese
he saw on the streets or in coffee shops listened now to rock 'n' roll
or rap music. They dressed like Westerners with jeans and T-shirts
bearing the names of American universities. They couldn't tell a
nihonto sword from a butter knife. They were too busy with money
and work to do the tea ceremony, or they sneered at it as part of
some ancient past. This made Jenkins very sad. Sometimes in his
journal, he wrote with almost no irony that he felt like the last true
Japanese.

Of one thing he was certain: the young Japanese were different from their fathers and mothers and grandparents. Television was rotting their brains, he thought, destroying even the most recent past. When Suzuki Junior came to the apartment for the first time, almost a year earlier, to tell Jenkins that he wanted him to move, the young man said: "Do you read all this old shit?"

Jenkins nodded and said simply, "Yes."

The young man smirked and took down a copy of a book by Nagai Kafu and stared at its pages as if it were written in Sanskrit. "Stupid," he said. "I can't even read this . . ."

"Then put it back on the shelf," Jenkins said coldly.

Suzuki Junior slipped the book back in place, and said, as he went to the door, "It will cost a lot of money to ship all of this junk home, won't it?"

Jenkins did not answer.

The truth was that he had no other home but this. He hadn't lived in America for more than forty years and now everybody that he knew there was dead. His family, his classmates, all the old soldiers. And even if he wanted to go back, he had so little money. Most of his earnings as a translator had gone to books; a social security check now came from the States each month but it barely covered rent and food. Even when his only sister had died the year before in California, he didn't go home for the funeral. The dollar had weakened so badly in the mid-eighties, the yen was so strong . . . He could not afford to fly to America, to crate up all of his precious possessions, to ship everything to a place he no longer knew. Not if he had to pay in yen. Even if he had money, begged or borrowed, even if he could fly to California to find some cheap place where he could live, he would have to leave his collections behind in the apartment in Kichijoji. A month could pass before he returned to pack them up. In the meantime, Suzuki Junior would simply walk in with some piece of legal paper and . . . No, Jenkins could not risk that. But he could not move elsewhere in Tokyo either. Who could afford to pay the rents of Tokyo now? Not an old man on a fixed income. Impossible. As the years had passed and Tokyo became more expensive, Suzuki-*san* never pressed him for an increase in rent; they were friends and Suzuki-*san* was an honorable man. But the son had the land fever. He had cajoled or threatened all of the other tenants into moving. Now Jenkins was the last. And Jenkins had nowhere to go.

3

In spite of his worst fear—the image he had of himself sitting on top of his collections in the rain—Jenkins tried to live his life according to the familiar routines. He shopped each morning, buying only what he needed for that day. In the afternoons, he read his books. In the evening, he wrote in his journal, in a strange personal mixture of English and *hiragana* script. He always stopped for tea. He went to bed early. And on Saturdays, he took the JR train to Ochanomizu station and walked for ten minutes to the bookstores of Kanda.

For Jenkins, this remained the most magical district of Tokyo. The high rents had forced too many booksellers to give up and retire, leaving the shops to sellers of sporting goods and the merchants of *manga*, the fat comic books of Japan. His friend Kiichiro had sold out and moved to Kyoto. Mizoguchi fell down dead one afternoon on the street outside his shop, and his son sold all the stock the following week. Others were forced to retire. But still there were dealers who owned their land and buildings and thus preserved enough of the old Kanda style to make Jenkins happy. The booksellers all knew him and sometimes saved him certain rare items. Most often these days, he could not afford to buy them. But he would hold these books to his face and breathe the holy aroma of old paper and dried glue. He would open their pages and read some lines. The booksellers gave him tea and a chair where he could sit, and Jenkins would vanish then for a few hours into his lost Japan.

Sometimes he let his book fall to his lap and he remembered the years after the war, when the survivors of the old middle class were so desperate for money and food that they sold off their libraries to

the shops of Kanda. What books he found in those years! Many
were made by hand, the paper flecked with wood grains, their pictures tinted with colored inks. Some were elegantly pornographic
guides to the Floating World. There were even great leatherbound
volumes in English, plunder from the conquests of Singapore and
the Philippines. At first, when his Japanese was crude, Jenkins
bought books as objects, for their shape and feel and odor. But later
he began to collect specific writers. He bought first editions and popular editions and paperback editions, sometimes as many as nine
copies of the same book, driven by an obsession for completion.
Some books were obviously not as good as others; but when he started on a specific writer, he wanted everything. He usually found it.

He loved Mori Ogai, for example, had copies of everything the
man had published, even his rare work, *Shibue Chusai*, which had
appeared as a serial in an Osaka newspaper in 1916. And he had
read many times *Okitsu Yagoemon no Isho*, the story inspired by the
ritual double suicide of General Nogi Maresuke and his wife after
the death of the Meiji emperor in 1912; like the *ronin*, they followed
their lord to the grave. Perhaps the act was foolish, even medieval,
but Nogi was true to a code that young men like Suzuki Junior now
dismissed as something out of old and boring movies. The only
code of the young was money.

Jenkins collected more than Ogai, of course. On his shelves he
had all of Tanizaki, all of Akutagawa, all of Kawabata, all of Natsume
Soseki, all of Dazai, along with dozens of others, some famous,
some obscure. His friends in the house in Kichijoji couldn't know
what it meant to Jenkins when he discovered in Kanda one Saturday
morning in 1963 the complete bound volumes of the journal *Shira-
kaba*, published during World War I. And how could he explain to
anyone, East or West, about his passion for Nagai Kafu? Old Kafu
the scribbler, lover of women, chronicler of Edo, forever alive in the
summer fogs of the Sumida River. Kafu was a prisoner of the same
nostalgia for his vanished Edo that Jenkins felt for the Tokyo that
began to disappear around the time of the 1964 Olympics. A sim-

pler Tokyo. One that was not so consumed by money and speculation and power. The Tokyo that belonged to Suzuki-*san*'s generation and not the generation of Suzuki Junior. Kafu called that city home.

In 1958, when Jenkins discovered Kafu's diaries in a store in Kanda and took them home, he read them continuously for sixty-three hours, without sleep. The diaries inspired him to begin his own journal, written in large accounting books. And now, lying alone in the empty building at night, thinking of Kafu, he often wondered what it would be like to have a place called home.

4

On this Saturday morning, Jenkins rose early as always. He had miso soup, white rice and egg. He gazed out at the street. He read for a while. At ten, he dressed, locked his door, went down the empty stairs to the street, and started for Kanda.

The day was bright with spring. He passed a *koban*, one of the small local police stations, and saw a cat purring on its roof and remembered the way the police used to come around with wooden cages for stray dogs and how in those days there were men employed full-time as rat catchers. Now all the rats were in the real estate business. He passed a boutique where the public baths used to be and that reminded him of the bar girl who lived briefly on the first floor of the house in Kichijoji in the 1950s. Otoyo. Yes, that was her name. Otoyo. She was as beautiful as any woman he'd ever seen. She always rose about one in the afternoon, and hurried down to the public baths, because the building had no hot water, not until years later. Then, freshly washed, she would come back and prepare for her evening's work. She had allowed him into her place for a few weeks, and in the afternoons, after making love, he would watch her do her makeup, applying base and powder and rouge until she became a different person. When she discovered that Jenkins was not rich, she broke off the affair in a cheerful and practical way; a year later he saw her playing small parts in movies, and a year after that he saw her smiling from the glossy pages of a society magazine, standing beside her unsmiling husband, a captain of industry with a broad nose and hairy hands. Thinking of her made him smile. He wasn't bitter about her calculations or her departure. In those days, survival was all. And besides, he remembered her body, her neck, the curve of her buttocks; those details were among the few proofs he could present to himself that he had not only read, but had also lived.

In the subway, he saw mothers and daughters together as he always did, but now the daughters were a full head taller than their mothers. The mothers grew up after the war too, when there were shortages, not enough protein, no milk. The daughters ate hamburgers from McDonald's. They were even taller than Jenkins. They walked boldly, with loose, long-legged strides, like Americans. He saw one girl with flawless skin, glossy black hair, hips curving in tight jeans. And then, suddenly, surprising even himself, Jenkins for the first time in years wanted a woman.

Absurd, he thought, coming up in Jimbocho. I'm sixty-eight years old. I'm small and lean, my skin is gullied by time, my eyes are weak from too much reading. These tall girls would laugh at me. He walked a few blocks, thinking about the bodies of women who had come in and out of his life, and then saw a cheap bar, with some girls inside. He paused, remembered stories in the newspapers about AIDS and how the *yakuza* brought these women from the Philippines or Thailand, how a lot of them were using drugs.

And he hurried away to the bookstores.

In one of the stores, the tiny man who owned the place handed him a battered copy of a book of stories by a woman named Higuchi Ichiyo. Jenkins was excited. He bowed, took a seat in the back of the store, sipped tea provided by the owner, and in his imagination slipped back in time into the Yoshiwara, where courtesans still blackened their teeth and the moat was dark under the moon and men arrived all night in rickshaws. When he came out of the book, it was almost five and Jenkins was alarmed. He said an abrupt goodbye to the bookshop owner and started for home.

He felt almost guilty now, staying away so long, a guilt that was mixed with an odd sense of dread. He would not have to explain his absence to a woman, of course, and that was sad. But his collections were so vulnerable. Like children. Thieves might enter the building. Suzuki Junior might arrive with the police and some legal writ and take them away. Thinking of women, and then reading about them, had eaten up so much time that he felt guilty of some awful infidelity. He cursed his books. And thought: No, they aren't my children, or my mistress; they're my lord; I serve them, they demand my loyalty, my time, my protection, my life.

He came up out of the subway and started for the house in Kichijoji. His dread began to build, obscure and formless. Up ahead, there was a stirring in the streets, traffic seemed backed up, kids were running.

He turned a corner and saw the fire engines, saw his building, saw flames near the roof, saw black smoke billowing from his apartment against the darkening sky. And across the street, talking to the police, was Suzuki Junior.

The young man was gesturing in a cool way, as if offering a theory to the police. Then he turned and saw Jenkins. He looked suddenly apprehensive, as if afraid that Jenkins might attack him, smash against him with his rage, in spite of the police, the helpless firemen, the gathering crowd and an old man's frailty.

But Jenkins did not move. He gazed at the upper floor of the building where he had lived for so long. And he saw the mushrooming smoke begin to shape the figures of the dead against the sky. There was Mr. Yamamoto, wearing a baseball cap. And there was Mr. Fukuzawa, happy and fat. And his lost wife with all the secret places of her body visible only to Jenkins. He watched and saw Lady Murasaki, as lovely as a lily, rising into the heavens too. And the woman who once shined shoes. And Suzuki-*san*. And even Otoyo. Beautiful Otoyo, waving and laughing and young. And there: he could see Nagai Kafu carrying his own precious diaries. He saw

Hiroshige. He saw rat-trappers and samurai. And Tanizaki. And Mori Ogai. All of them. They were all there, escaping from the books and the diaries and the bound volumes of ancient journals, rising from the ruins of his lost Tokyo and from everything that had made his life a life.

Slowly at first, and then dashing past the firemen, leaping over hoses, splashing through water, ignoring shouts, Jenkins ran to join them. His heart was bursting with love and duty and communion as he plunged into the flames.

The Blue Stone

1

Buxton was the only customer in the small British-style pub. Perched on a stool at the bar, he was pretending to read a newspaper, the English edition of the *Yomiuri Shimbun*, but often paused, shaping unspoken words that had nothing to do with the pages in his hands, and gazed out at the late afternoon rain falling on the Ginza. Syrupy ballads played on a tape machine. The fat Japanese bartender looked sad and stolid. Buxton smoked one cigarette, then another, sipped a tepid beer, lit a third cigarette and then saw her at last, moving through the rain-lashed array of bobbing umbrellas. Her name was Aya. Her hair was covered with a plastic rain hat and her eyes were fixed on the rain-slick pavement as she moved among the other pedestrians with what Buxton thought was a thrilling elegance. Aya. So beautiful . . . Come to me, Aya, he thought. Now. And then added, No, Aya, don't, Aya, please stay away, Aya. Keep going. Take the subway home. Spare me this meeting. Forget me. Let me forget you.

Then she was slipping in the door, smiling at him in a shy and tentative way. He stood up, as she removed the rain hat and unbuttoned her coat, and he took her hand and moved with her to a corner table. She smelled of soap and rain. He helped her with the coat, hung it on a wall peg, and without asking her (for he knew) he ordered a whiskey and soda from the bartender and another beer for himself. He took the drinks and sat beside her and brushed her cheek with a kiss. She stared at him, then smiled in an uneasy way.

"You're worried about something," she said, in her plain, un-accented English.

"Yes," he said, and shrugged, and fumbled for a cigarette. "Yes, I'm worried."

She gazed at him, the intelligent eyes peering at him, saying nothing, waiting. He inhaled deeply. After so many years, she still could make him squirm just by looking at him.

"Aya, I—" He paused, trying to slow himself, to make what he must say sound less drastic. But he couldn't find other words. "Aya, I'm leaving Tokyo. They're bringing me back to the home office."

She said, "Oh."

And nothing else.

She turned to her right, away from him, and stared out through the front window at the rain. Three schoolgirls giggled under one umbrella and were gone. A gaunt Westerner stopped before the window, holding a pulpy newspaper over his head, gazed inside, then hurried on. Traffic was stalled, cars and trucks looking welded together. Aya's smooth brow crinkled, then smoothed again. A muscle jumped beside her mouth. She didn't look at Buxton.

"It's considered a promotion," he said. "And it is. It really is. They want me to be part of upper management. It's a great break for me, in some ways. A real chance . . ." He paused, smiled. "But the truth? I think they want to save money."

"Yes," she said.

"It costs them a ton to keep an office here," he said. "You know the problem. Rents for offices and apartments, extra money for the employees, the usual. A lot of American companies are leaving. It's been in all the papers." He glanced at the bar, where his copy of the *Yomiuri* lay untouched. "They're trying to blame the Japanese, but the fact is they—"

She looked at him then. "I don't need to hear a speech," she said crisply. "I don't need to hear someone's newspaper column. You're going. They want you to go and you're going. There's nothing else to say, is there?"

He mashed his butt into a plastic ashtray. The door opened and two salarymen entered, gazed indifferently at Buxton and Aya, and sat down at the bar, talking loudly about sewing machines and the labor unions of Taiwan.

"It wasn't my idea," Buxton said.

"I know," Aya said, a faint bitter tone in her voice.

"Maybe you *don't* know," Buxton said. "I want you to be sure. I want you to know that I absolutely don't *want* this. I argued against it. I sent a detailed memo to the home office. I told them very clearly that I want to stay here. I did."

"Did you say in your amazingly detailed memo that you had a mistress who was a married woman?"

"No," he said with some heat. "Don't play games with me over this, Aya. I'm serious."

She smiled in the subtlest way. "Of course."

She turned away and her hand went almost involuntarily into her bag. She removed something that he couldn't see. He sipped his beer and then looked at her again and her eyes were brimming with tears.

"Please don't cry," he whispered.

"I don't want to," she said.

"It will only make things worse," he said. He squeezed her hand, shifted the tone of his voice. "We've been apart before."

"But this is different," she said. "This time you're going away for good."

"No," he lied.

"Yes. This time you'll go forever."

He reached for her hand. Her fingers were closed in a fist. Gently, he pried them open. In the palm of her hand, damp and warm, was a smooth blue stone.

2

"You remember that day?" she said.

"Of course," he said.

"I don't believe you."

"It was February in New York," he said, telling her what she knew. "Nixon was still the president. We were still fighting in Vietnam. You were twenty-one."

"You were twenty-eight," she said.

"You were a student at Cooper Union, wanting to be a painter."

"You were a painter," she said, as if reciting a sad catechism. "The first one I'd ever met."

"I wasn't any good."

"Not true," she said. "You were good."

"But not good enough."

They were side by side now in the bed in his small apartment, high above the streets of Shinjuku. The room was shadowed with dark grays. Cold rain lashed the sliding glass doors leading to the balcony.

"You had a car that day," she whispered, holding the blue stone.

"A '68 Chevy."

"Black, with red upholstery," she said.

"And white-walled tires," he said, laughing.

A pause.

"We drove out to Long Island," he said.

"It was a Saturday," she said. "Rainy and gray. Like today."

"It began to snow," he said. He took her hand and felt the blue stone. It was warm. He held it tightly, as her warmth passed into him, here on this cold day in Tokyo, a long way from the flat empty reaches of Long Island.

"You kept on driving through the snow," she said. "After a while, we were the only car on the road. The Eagles were singing on the radio. That was their year. They were singing every other song on every other station. . . . We couldn't see anything before us or to the sides or behind us."

"Finally, I pulled off the highway," he whispered. "We drove on side roads, the snow storm roaring in off the Atlantic."

"I said, 'Take me to the Hotel California,'" she said.

"But the hotels were all closed."

"And the lights were out in all the houses."

"The summer places were abandoned," he said.

"And then the snow eased, grew softer, and we were beside the bay," she said.

"The water was frozen," he said. "We got out of the car. The snow dissolved in your hair. I wanted to paint you that way, as beautiful as anyone in the world has ever been. Except that I knew I didn't have the talent."

"You began to pick up stones at the shore of the bay," she said. "You began to throw them across the ice."

"And then I found the blue stone," he said. "It was too beautiful to throw. Blue and smooth and perfect."

"You gave it to me. . . ."

She lay there, the sheet pulled to her chin. Her hand went to his and took the stone away from him again.

"Do you remember what you said to me?" she said.

He didn't answer.

"Well, I do," she said. "You told me I should carry this stone with me for the rest of my life. You said it was the symbol of our love, that it always existed and always would exist, permanent and pure. You pressed it in my hand. You said you would love me forever. You kissed me so hard I thought my lips were bruised." A pause. "I believed you." Another pause. "Oh, how I believed you."

She stared without expression at the ceiling. Outside, the rain sounded harder against the windows, like hail or sand. She touched his face.

"We'll never make love again, will we?" she said.

3

Aya had carried the blue stone with her to Mexico that summer, while the Americans were cheering the departure of Richard Nixon and the war ran down in Vietnam. It was in her pocket when she

and Buxton climbed the pyramid of the sun in Teotihuacán. She
had it with her when she first was pulled into the noisy murals of
Rivera and Orozco and when she dove into the rich reds and lumi-
nous yellows of Tamayo. On that trip, she and Buxton stayed
together in a bright high-ceilinged room in the Hotel Majestic,
overlooking the Zocalo in Mexico City. There she saw the way the
Indian cleaning women stared at her high cheekbones and lustrous
black hair and almond eyes and seemed to be wondering: is she one
of us? And there one midnight Buxton first asked her to marry him.
She laughed and said she would think about it. What was there to
think about? he said. And she said: I'm twenty-one, I'm too young,
I'm not a complete person yet, I want to be a painter, I want to learn
my craft, you are from America, I'm from Japan; too much to think
about now, wait.

They waited through another year, while Buxton painted less
and less. He always said later that Mexico had ruined him. Mexico
and the art of Japan. Or so he told Aya. At first, full of the swagger of
youth, he told her that all that old stuff was only another challenge.
But he wasn't afraid. He'd rise to the damned challenge, go up
against the so-called old masters the way Cassius Clay went against
Sonny Liston. One night while Aya was there, he tacked a Rivera
poster to the wall of his cramped studio, laughed out loud, and said:
come on, old man, let's rumble! Come on, you big ugly bear! But
that winter, everything he tried to do on a grander scale seemed
only a kind of painted rhetoric. He painted the walls of his apartment on Houston Street, filling every square inch with writhing figures that screamed against injustice and tyranny. In his drawings, he
tried to merge the colors of Tamayo with the space of Hokusai (or
so he explained to Aya) in order to transform the zeitgeist. He didn't
really know what the zeitgeist was, but everyone he knew used the
word and so did he. On his walls, he crowded his compositions with
faces from newspapers and magazines, breaking up the images,
splashing paint around to fill in the gaps, trying not to be Rivera but
obsessed with him too. At three in the morning, he was always sure

he'd made a masterpiece; when he woke up in the mornings and looked at what he'd done, it all looked dead.

Meanwhile, Aya's work got better. She lost interest in the painting of others, after seeing too much of it in the galleries of New York, most of it slovenly when it was not fraudulent or corrupt. Her own work became simpler, cleaner, more elegant. In Japan she'd learned almost nothing about Zen Buddhism; in New York, the downtown crowd spoke about Zen as casually as if it were part of baseball. The road to the gardens of Kyoto passed through Greenwich Village. Now she talked of becoming a designer. Of using her abilities to make the world simpler and more beautiful. As beautiful, she told Buxton, as the blue stone.

"That would be a glorious world, wouldn't it?" she said.

And Buxton laughed in a cynical way. Later he would say that he was one of the moral casualties of the sixties; after seeing so much ruin and disappointment, he could no longer imagine a world that got better. At twenty, he was prepared to die to improve the world; as he approached thirty, he considered that old faith an embarrassment, a forlorn hope, a juvenile delusion. "Almost everything we believed in turned to shit," he said, perhaps too often. "Even rock 'n' roll." He had read his Voltaire, and like Candide he was now convinced that the only solution was to tend one's private garden. But in that secret garden, he wanted Aya.

He, in fact, wanted her beyond the limits of common sense. As he painted less and less, he devoted more and more of his energy and imagination to their relationship, and within a few months had succeeded in completely frightening her. He asked her every day to marry him. When they were apart, he called her every few hours, whispering, pleading, and demanded an accounting of her movements if she wasn't home. He made pictures of her, great churning Rivera-like assemblages of images and longings and borrowings. As she reached in her work for simplicity, Buxton insisted on complexity, in art and life. "You want me too much," she said to him one night. "You want to occupy me, body and soul, not just love me."

He protested; that wasn't true; he wanted to love her, not own her. But even in his fury and passion, he realized that she was, of course, right. He just couldn't bring himself to admit it. Not then. Not in the heat of argument. His pride wouldn't allow him to admit any weakness at all. That was in May. In June she graduated with honors from Cooper Union, and two days later flew home to Japan.

He wrote to her, long passionate letters in which he finally admitted that he had put too much pressure on her, had demanded too much, had indeed treated her as if he were a one-man occupying army. But still, he wrote in the letters, he loved her. Couldn't that be a starting point? He would control his demands, he would tame his possessiveness. Please, he said. And if she didn't want him now, he wrote, he would wait for her. Just like one of those guys in all those songs. Whenever she wanted to come back to New York, he would be there.

She sent a few replies to his letters. They were lean, noncommittal, decorated with small drawings of her cat and her friends. Then, two of his letters went unanswered, and another, and then one of the first two came back, with a message stamped across the front saying in Japanese that this person had moved and left no forwarding address.

That was it. Aya was gone. Out of his life. Or so Buxton thought. A year later, he gave up painting for good and joined an advertising agency as a layout man. He discovered that he was a giant among pygmies. Or so he thought. And so his progress taught him. In two swift years, he went from layout man to art director to what the agency called Vice President of Creative Affairs. He mastered the language of advertising and spoke it as if it were his native tongue. He won awards. He was written about in the trade magazines. He almost never thought about Aya anymore. Too busy. Too successful. Oh, there was a campaign he created once around the theme of the Zen of Driving; it was designed to combat the arrival of the first successful Japanese cars and while he was writing the copy he thought of Aya and his foolish passion and felt briefly mortified. But only briefly. In his fifth year, he left the agency, borrowed a million dollars on the strength of his reputation, and started his own company. And six months after that, he married a woman he'd met at a sales convention three days earlier.

The marriage was a disaster. When it ended, a few painful years later, Buxton had lost his agency, his reputation and his bank account. None of this was private. The story was in all the trades and even made some of the gossip columns in the dailies. Buxton went to Europe for a month and when he came home he made a few phone calls to his few remaining friends, registered with one of those professional headhunters who place executive talent, and waited. For nine long months, he didn't work. He didn't paint either. He did almost nothing, except play old movies on his VCR and stare out at the New York skyline from his apartment on the Brooklyn side of the harbor.

Then one Friday morning, he got the call from Freddie Cotter at Sanders & Dancer.

"Hey, old tiger," Cotter said affectionately, "how'd you like to go to Japan?"

The firm of Sanders & Dancer was one of the three biggest American advertising agencies. They never won awards for elegance of vision, for wit or for style; they just earned millions of dollars. Cotter said they were opening an office in Tokyo and wanted him to be the No. 2 man. A comedown perhaps, for a guy who'd once been so hot. A sure sign that nobody else wanted the job. Hell, even Cotter had an apologetic tone when he made the offer.

But Buxton immediately thought of Aya.

"When do I leave?" he said.

4

"When you came to Japan, why did you look for me?" she said now, dressing in the dark bedroom.

"You know why," he said. "I told you before: I love you. I never stopped loving you."

"But you knew I was married."

"Yes. Of course."

"And you knew I would never leave my husband."

"That's what you said to me. That first time. After I was here a month. After I found you . . . Yes, you said that to me, and I listened, but I didn't believe you."

She was dressed now, chic and cool. For the first time, she took one of his cigarettes. She lit it and then walked out through the bedroom door into the dark living room. Buxton walked behind her and saw that the room had an odd bright glow.

"Snow," she said. "Snow . . ."

The rain had turned to great fat round flakes, falling through the darkened sky.

"Snow. . . ," she whispered, and began sliding open the balcony door. She stepped outside. The city had a hushed, almost reverent feeling to it now. She took a drag on the cigarette and let the smoke drift into the dark air. Buxton held onto the balcony railing. Before them, entire buildings vanished in the swirling whiteness. He put an arm around her.

"We walked along the edge of the bay," he said.

"The stone was warm in my hand."

"And we saw the house on the point," he said. "Boarded up, snow drifting on the deck, ice at the base."

"I climbed the stairs to the deck," she said. "The blue stone in my hand."

"I came up the stairs behind you," he said. "The snow grew denser. I tried the doors."

"And found one open."

"There was no alarm," he said.

"We went inside. It smelled of an old summer afternoon. We sat down, wet and cold . . ."

"And made love on the floor," he said. "Like savages."

"And later ran into the storm, naked," she said, "laughing and crazy. The snow against our bodies."

"Your nipples were hard in the cold. There was a faint blue vein in your breast."

"We made love in the snow."

"With steam coming from our bodies and the snow warm and our faces hot."

"Nobody around for a million miles."

"A long time ago," he said.

Now she was weeping. The snow fell steadily on Tokyo.

"I don't want you to go," she said.

"I must," he said. "I have a life to live."

The snow was dissolving in her hair. As it did once, long ago.

"You *want* to leave me, don't you?" she said. "You *want* to leave Tokyo, to start your career again, to become a big player again, to—"

"You have a *husband*," he said bitterly. "You have a *child*. You have a goddamned career *too*. You—"

"Stop," she said, wiping tears on her sleeve.

He put his arm around her, held her close to him. The snow was blinding now, the city as silent as death.

"Come with me," he said. "Get a divorce, live with me in New York." He breathed out hard. "Come with me."

She eased away from him, then abruptly faced him, her makeup smeared by tears and snow.

"No," she said. "No. No." And then, biting her lip, her eyes glistening, her hair wet, she turned and hurled the blue stone out into the whiteness. She paused, head cocked, eyes widening, as if expecting to hear it land somewhere far below. But there was no sound except her breathing. And his.

She turned to him once more, whispered goodbye, and walked back through the apartment to the door. Buxton didn't watch her go. He heard the door close. But he just stood there, staring into the falling snow, his face frozen, his hands like ice, hoping that somewhere deep in the blinding whiteness he would see the lost road beside the bay and the beach house where the door was unlocked and her nipples would be hard against his chest and he would hold her hand, their fingers meshed and laced, and pressed between their palms would be the warm blue stone.

"Come with me," he said out loud.

But there was no answer from the whirling snow-thick city.

Samurai

1

Jimmy Ferguson lived in Japan before he ever saw the country. At fifteen, in a small movie house on the Upper West Side of Manhattan, he first saw Akira Kurosawa's movie *Seven Samurai*. He had never seen a Japanese film before nor heard the Japanese language. He didn't know what a samurai was. But the film, as he told his friends back home in Queens, "just blew me away." They looked at him as if he were getting very strange.

Ferguson wasn't content with that single viewing. He saw the movie four times in three days, sitting alone because his friends refused to join him, and in the following months he sought out other Kurosawa films: *Rashomon* and *Ikiru* and *Yojimbo*. They were playing in New York that summer as part of some festival, and Jimmy Ferguson would sit in the dark, transported to an exotic country, a Japan that was becoming more real for him by the day. He was impressed by the actor Toshiro Mifune for all the obvious reasons—his explosive physical movement, his handsome face, his humor; an article in *The New York Times* described him as the Japanese John Wayne, and Jimmy Ferguson said yes, that's true, but he's even better; after all, could John Wayne use a sword the way Mifune did?

But slowly his real hero became the actor Takashi Shimura. Across that summer and into the fall (when he saw revivals of *Stray Dogs* and *Drunken Angel*), Shimura began to exist in his mind as the father he did not have.

The young man's own father had been killed in Vietnam when

Jimmy Ferguson was eight months old; he existed only as a fading photograph on a mantel. Jimmy's mother was sweet and caring and supportive of his whims and fancies, but she'd never married again and Ferguson needed a father. He found that father in Shimura. The man's eyes were full of intelligence, compassion, endurance, and wisdom. He was always firm and strong when life was at its toughest. And Jimmy Ferguson was certain that if he ever behaved in a foolish or stupid or careless way, Shimura would point out his errors, urge him never to repeat them, and then forgive him. The essential point would always be the same: learn from your mistakes or you cannot be a man.

This was not a passing stage in Jimmy Ferguson's young life. Every year he went to the Kurosawa revivals; they were like journeys home. But there was more. He began to read in the public library about Japan, to look first at travel books and large glossy portfolios of photographs, trying to understand the country and its history and the codes by which its people lived. He talked to his mother about the samurai, about the intricate moral and professional rules that governed their lives. He convinced his friends to practice swordplay with him, using wooden poles or broom handles. His friends soon tired of this; they preferred to spend their time on baseball or girls. So Jimmy Ferguson practiced alone on the rooftop of his building or in the football field at school, where at noon the tackling dummies were not used. In the final years of high school, he wrote term papers about Japanese culture, and always earned an A, primarily because the teachers knew almost nothing about the subject, but also because of the boy's evident passion. The boy tried to make these papers as strong and perfect as possible, writing draft after draft, because in his room at night, as he labored over them, he always felt the steady, ghostly presence of Takashi Shimura.

"You know more about Japan than I know about America," his mother said one day, when the boy was in his final year of high school. "I wonder about you, boy."

"I want to go there some day," he said.

She laughed.

"Why not?" she said. "Your father was there, too, when he was young."

Her mood abruptly changed, the smile vanished. The young man hugged her and said, "Don't, Mom."

"I'm sorry. . . ."

"It's a long way from Vietnam," he said.

"Not far enough."

2

When he was eighteen, Jimmy Ferguson went to Columbia University on a scholarship. Jimmy chose Columbia because it had a splendid Asian Studies department. Every morning, as he traveled by subway from Queens to the upper Manhattan campus, he was possessed by his vision. He would first complete his undergraduate studies, of course, but he didn't need to wait to learn more about Japan. The university's library was fabulous, full of antique volumes he could never find in the used bookstores of the city; he would take his time, consume those books, learn everything, lay a solid foundation, and eventually he would enter the Asian Studies department and become a brilliant scholar of Japan.

His mother went along with him on almost everything. For a Halloween costume party at the university, she bought him a *happi*, a loose kimono which allowed him to practice swordplay with even greater fluidity. In his room that night, dressed in his *happi*, he posed and strutted and barked words in bogus Japanese, acting like Mifune but wondering what Shimura would think of him. At the Halloween party, he did not drink; no samurai would allow himself to look foolish in front of strangers. And with the young women, he was grave and reserved, standing with his arms folded while the other young men, dressed as monsters or vampires or cowboys, got roaring drunk. Naturally, most of them thought he was odd. Even the young women. Once again, Jimmy Ferguson went home alone.

He accepted his isolation with stoic grace. The university was otherwise glorious. He studied hard at his undergraduate courses, but also found time for his own passionate concerns. He delved into the history of Asian nations, read histories of Japan, listened to tapes of the Japanese language. Then one afternoon in the main reading room at the Butler Library, he met Masayo.

She was sitting at a long, blonde-wood table in the high-ceilinged reading room. There was a stack of books beside her on the table and she was writing in a notebook with furious concentration. She had a plain face, without makeup, and wore thick glasses that made her look scholarly. Ferguson sat down at the same table. She looked up, smiled in a shy way, and returned to her books. Jimmy Ferguson opened the book he was studying, a treatise on Zen Buddhism by D.T. Suzuki. He noticed that she was studying books on Thomas Jefferson, stopping, scribbling notes in a Japanese script, then cross-indexing material in the other books. He was struggling with his own book, trying to understand concepts written in vague prose.

Then he cleared his throat and said: "You must be studying American history."

She smiled. "Yes. American civilization." Her smile transformed her face, and Ferguson thought: she's beautiful. "Jefferson is so interesting," she said, in formal English that had a faintly British rhythm. "He was very intelligent and yet he kept slaves. He had a slave woman as his mistress. It was such a . . . contradiction?"

An hour later, they were in a coffee shop on the campus. She was twenty-three, a graduate student, attending Columbia for a year. She lived in a noisy apartment with three other women students on 116th Street, a few blocks away. She was trying hard to improve her English, she said, and Jimmy Ferguson said, in crude Japanese, "It's very good." She told him how to say the phrase better, made him repeat it, laughing over the coffee, and teaching him other phrases. He walked her home. They agreed to see a movie on Friday (although she seemed very nervous about this), and when he saw her again, he was convinced he was in love.

They saw each other every day after that, practicing English and Japanese in almost equal proportions. He was shocked to learn that she had never seen *Seven Samurai*, did not really know who this Akira Kurosawa was, so he took her to a screening at a multiplex in Soho. She was impressed. "How did you like Shimura?" he said, and she laughed and said she much preferred the thin silent actor with the quick sword. "Well," he said with a smile, "at least you didn't say Mifune." He held her hand as they walked back to her apartment from the subway. She invited him up for tea. The apartment was silent; her roommates had gone to Washington for the weekend. She prepared green tea. They sipped it in silence. And then made love. Ferguson was a virgin and thought he would explode. When they were finished, Masayo cried and cried.

3

Suddenly, it was June. And one sultry Sunday afternoon in the apartment, with her roommates again off on some convenient errands, Masayo abruptly told Jimmy Ferguson that she must return home. Her year in New York was over and she had to go back to her life. He pleaded with her to stay, to live with him, to marry him. This made her cry again. No, she said, no, she couldn't do that. And then it got worse. She told him that she wanted to be apart from him for a week, to study for her exams, to finish her paper on Henry Ford. He said he would help her. She said no, she must be alone. He started to protest again, to tell her that he couldn't stand not seeing her, and then he felt Takashi Shimura watching him. Ferguson became instantly stoic, nodded his assent, and said he would call her after the exams were over. At the door, she kissed him tenderly and turned away, crying once more, and closed the door.

He was true to his word. But when he called a week later, one of the roommates answered the telephone. Masayo was not there.

"Do you know where she is?" Ferguson asked.

"Yes," the young woman said. "She's gone back to Japan."

He did not handle this news in a stoic way. For one long day, he remained in bed, with the door of his room locked. He buried his face in his pillow and wept. He felt sick and did not eat. Finally his mother knocked hard on his door and he rose slowly and pulled on his *happi*, which he used as a bathrobe. He opened the door and she stared at him for a long moment.

"Okay," she said. "What's her name?"

He told her, struggling for control, and she led him to the kitchen and told him to eat, and asked questions and listened to his stumbling answers. He poked at his food, explaining about the Japanese girl he'd never told her about before (for a samurai could not discuss such matters with his mother) and how he loved her. His mother prepared a pot of coffee and poured two cups and then sat down and faced Jimmy Ferguson across the kitchen table.

"There's only one thing you can do," she said.

"What's that?" he said.

"Go and get her."

4

And so he prepared for his trip to his other country. First, a friend in the administration office found Masayo's address in Tokyo. Then Ferguson made a deal with his mother: he would study hard and pass his exams, then she would lend him the money for the airplane and a week in a hotel. He would pay her back over the following year, from money earned in a job at the university cafeteria. She agreed with a patient sigh. He found a travel agent near Columbia who got him a cheap ticket and a reservation in a second-class hotel. With the ticket in hand, he was able to get a passport in one day and then went to the Japanese consulate for a visa. He took his exams at Columbia and was sure he did well. That week, with everything in place, he started writing a letter to Masayo, to tell her that he was coming, but then decided not to finish it. If she knew he was coming, she might panic, send him a telegram, tell him to stay at home in his own country.

No, he would just go.

Show up on her doorstep.

Prove to her that he was not speaking empty words to her. Prove that even though she was five years older than he was, he was a serious man. He was, in fact, a kind of samurai.

The day of departure arrived. His mother offered to drive him to the airport. No, he said (thinking of Shimura); he would take a taxi (thinking, a man must go alone to meet his fate). "Don't go anywhere else except Tokyo," his mother said, close to tears. And he promised her that he wouldn't go near Vietnam.

All the way across the Pacific, he studied maps of Tokyo, trying to locate her house. He couldn't find the street on any map and his stomach churned with anxiety. Then he talked to one of the stewardesses and showed her the address and she looked at it, examined the map, and used a yellow marker to chart the route on the Tokyo subway system. Only then did Ferguson relax. He dozed through the Arnold Schwarzenegger movie, watched the shorts about passport control and customs, read some of a Suzuki book on Zen, again studied his maps. Most of the time, he dozed, his mind teeming with visions of Masayo's smiling face as she opened the door and saw him.

The arrival went well, except that Ferguson was very tired. He took the airport bus, which stopped a block from his hotel. Every face he saw was Japanese, and he now understood how Masayo must have felt in certain parts of New York. He registered, paid cash in advance (for he had no credit cards), and went to his room. It was late in the day. He decided that he'd better sleep and go to find Masayo in the morning. He didn't want to show up exhausted. He didn't want to look drained or heartbroken. He stared out the window, looking at signs in *kanji*, at rooftops, at people hurrying along in the street, and then as if a wave had rushed through him, he realized where he was.

"Tokyo," he whispered. "I can't believe it. Tokyo . . ."

He unpacked and washed and then lay down. He fell asleep immediately.

When he woke up, the city was still dark. He could hear the sound of tires moving on wet streets. He looked out and saw that a fine drizzle was falling. He glanced at his watch and tried to figure out the time. Twenty minutes after two. He couldn't go calling on anyone at this hour. He lay down again and read the Suzuki book, hoping for some blank Zen screen in his mind. After a paragraph, he was asleep again.

He was wakened by the sound of a truck backfiring. The morning light was gray and the rain was still falling. It was about half past seven. He showered and dressed and then looked again at the map. He went downstairs and changed a $50 bill for yen at the front desk and bought a *Japan Times*. In the coffee shop, he glanced at the world news. I'm here, he thought. I'm in Japan, I'm in Tokyo, I'm eighteen years old and I'm in this place on the far side of the world. I did it. And the woman I love is here and I'm going to find her and take her home.

5

The subway was two blocks away. Using the map, he changed from one line to another, the cars crowded with businessmen and schoolchildren and women going to jobs. Twenty minutes later, he saw his stop and got off, feeling more nervous than ever. He came up into a part of Tokyo where high rises climbed above two-story buildings in a jumble of styles. The warm drizzle was still falling. Ferguson soon discovered that in this district the map didn't help. He couldn't find the street. He wandered around for a while, as people under umbrellas hurried past him, all of them distracted and private. He realized that he was the only Westerner on the street and that he was taller than almost everyone he passed, except one man in a running suit. Ferguson used the *Japan Times* as an umbrella and hurried along, rehearsing Japanese phrases that he hoped would help him find his way. But the rain was driving people too quickly; their umbrellas were used like shields and he felt that stopping any of them would be an intrusion. At one point, he saw an elevated train in the distance and remembered the scene in *High and Low* where Mifune had to squeeze the briefcase with the ransom money through a small opening in the men's room window of the bullet train; and how in that movie Shimura was a senior detective who said almost nothing, yet forced the younger detectives to perform at the top of their skills.

Ferguson turned a corner and came upon a *koban*, one of the small storefront police stations he'd seen in travel books. There were two policemen inside, one old, one young. He went in and showed them the address and his map and the older man told him very politely in Japanese how to go there, pointing with pencils at lines in the map, gesturing with his hands at the rainy streets, then repeating the directions with the aid of a huge blown-up map of the district. The younger policeman watched carefully as if absorbing a lesson in giving directions to foreigners. The policemen bowed, Ferguson bowed and thanked them in his hesitant Japanese. They bowed again. He started walking in the rain.

The house was on a side street that climbed a hill. All the houses here were connected, like houses back in Queens, but each looked different. At Masayo's address, there was a front gate leading to a small garden and a two-story house. The windows were obscured with shades or curtains. He tried the gate and it was open. He paused, struggling with a sudden panic, then settled, breathed deeply, and walked in. A dog barked somewhere. He stuffed the wet newspaper in his pocket and then knocked on the door.

He waited a while, and then knocked again.

The door opened. A Japanese man stood there, about thirty years old, tall, wearing a short-sleeved shirt and trousers. His feet were in slippers. He looked like the young detective in *High and Low*.

"Hello," Ferguson said in stumbling Japanese, "I'm looking for Masayo."

The man said, "She's not here."

"Do you expect her back?" Ferguson said.

"Yes. She went to the store. Who are you?"

"A friend from New York. From Columbia."

"Oh, good, good," the man said, suddenly smiling. "Do you want to come in? I'm Masayo's husband."

Jimmy Ferguson froze. The man said something else but Ferguson didn't hear the words.

"No, no, I was just, uh, passing by," he said in English. Then switched to Japanese. "I'll call her. Thank you. Thank you."

He bowed and hurried away into the rain. A wind was rising. The rain fell more heavily. He saw nothing, moving down the hill, and he wanted to cry, to sit down in the rain, to sob and writhe and fall apart. But then he thought of Takashi Shimura. He saw the great man's eyes gazing at him: stern, humane, stoic. And he began to walk more slowly, holding himself erect, striding through the rain in his imaginary city, a long way from home.

Running for Home

1

Suddenly, as he turned to face the window, Scanlon felt that his hotel room had been transformed into a prison. To be sure, it was a prison where he could drink a bottle of Kirin beer, where he could call for room service, where the bed was clean and pictures of birds adorned the walls. There were no bars on the windows. But it was a prison in his mind, a place from which he could not leave until his sentence was served.

"I'm alone," he said out loud, gazing at the lights of Tokyo, the passing cars, the hooked sliver of the moon. "Totally, fucking alone." Then, as if needing to speak English, he spoke some more: "I'm a *gaijin* in Japan. That's what they call foreigners here and as long as I stay, that's all I'll ever be: *gaijin*. But I'm more than that. I'm thirty-two years old and I play baseball for a living and I don't love it anymore."

The words sounded at once tentative and final. He thought: do I really mean what I'm saying? Or am I dramatizing myself again? Hey, that would not be new. I've dramatized myself all my life. To women. To two wives. To other players. To sportswriters and fans and taxi drivers. Sometimes—a *lot* of times—I brought the drama to the playing field: a steal of home, a triple with two on, bottom of the ninth. But usually it was just words. Am I doing it again? No, the words are true: I don't love it anymore. I don't love trotting out on a field to play ball. Not anymore.

He opened his wallet and took out the old photograph, laminated to protect it from time and sweat. In the photograph he was eleven years old and standing with his father, who was holding a baseball bat and showing him how to cock it and hit an unseen ball. The boy was not looking at the bat (though he remembered it clearly now, an Enos Slaughter model, 32 ounces); he was looking at his father. The father he so loved and so feared and so desperately wanted to please. Now, a *gaijin* in Japan, far from the hard, bright California sunshine, he was staring at his father again, wishing he could pick up the telephone and ask him for advice. The way he did all through the minor leagues, even into the first seasons in the majors; as he did right up to the moment his father's car went off that road in Malibu Canyon. Scanlon wanted to talk to him now. Not about his swing. Not about hitting left-handed pitching. About his life.

But his father wasn't there anymore and neither was the bat, which Scanlon had broken against his father's fastball when he was fifteen. All he had now was that snapshot of a year when he was innocent and in love with a game of ball. The picture had been his talisman for so long; it was a reminder of how it had all begun. Now the photograph of his beginnings seemed to be just another part of his past. Like the great seasons and the good stats. A mere document. And like the stats in the record book, it might verify a vanished season but it couldn't ever describe them. He had carried the photograph with him to Little League games, through high school tournaments, into the low minors and up to the Big Leagues. That photograph had traveled with him to all the scary cities of America. Looking at it before a game, he would be filled with the tension of competition, the coiled spring of arrogance, anger and fear that could only be relieved by playing ball. If he played ball right, the man in the picture would love him. He always knew that. If he failed, if he gave less than a hundred percent, if he dogged it, the man in the picture would turn his back and walk away in disgust. Now the picture was with him in Japan. Right here at the end. He wished he didn't have the goddamned photograph. He wished he had his father.

The door.

Someone at the door.

He put his beer down and walked to the door and then paused. Thinking, Don't answer. It's probably Tabuchi, the team interpreter, a kind of ambassador to the *gaijin*. He was a nice fella, but he spoke for the manager, not the players. And Scanlon didn't want to hear from Mr. Nakadai, the manager. He didn't want to apologize, and he didn't want to hear anything from the man. Fuck him. He was through with him and through with baseball. Still, he was a grown man now. He couldn't hide in a hotel room, even if that room felt like a goddamned jail.

"Yes?" Scanlon said.

"It's me," came the muffled voice. "Buddy."

Scanlon opened the door and Buddy Heater walked in, his black face gleaming in the light, his big thick body straining against a Hawaiian shirt that was a size too small. He was the other *gaijin* on the team, a first baseman now, still able to hit the long ball. His legs were shot, which is why he no longer roamed through center field. In the late innings of close games, they had to use a pinch runner for him, but he always played. In the States, Buddy Heater was forgotten; here he was famous. For good reason. Heater had been in Japan for four seasons. He spoke Japanese and had a Japanese wife in the town where they played and a beautiful Japanese house there and Japanese fans who loved him. Even here in Tokyo, where they were the visiting team, the fans waited at the end of the games to have him sign their programs. Scanlon had been here now for three months and nobody loved him at all.

"Well, old buddy," Heater said, "you really fucked up this time."

"*I* fucked up?" Scanlon said. "Are you nuts? I didn't fuck up. *He* fucked up."

Buddy Heater smiled and took a beer from the ice bucket and opened it. Scanlon thought: You've come to do business, haven't you?

"He's the manager," Heater said. "He can take you out of a game whenever he wants."

"In the middle of an inning? While I'm in left field and the fans are screaming? He takes me out like *that*?"

"He thought you didn't try for the ball."

"Bullshit. I came for it. I just couldn't reach the son of a bitch."

There was an awkward silence. Scanlon felt the humiliation of his removal flood through him again. Heater looked at him coldly.

"Come on, man, you let it fall."

"You agree with him?"

"I said you let it *fall*," Heater said. "You dive, maybe you get it. Maybe the inning's over. Maybe we win. You let it fall, the run scores, they go ahead and an inning later, we lose."

"You've been here too long, Buddy," Scanlon said. "You're taking their side."

"I want to win," Heater said. "So do they. If that's taking their side, fuck it, I'll take their side."

"You think I dogged it?"

"Yeah."

"Is that what Nakadai thinks too?"

"Why don't you ask *him*?"

2

Nakadai was a grave, quiet man in his early sixties, with a lean face and the eyes of a hawk. He looked the way a manager should look—absolutely focused—and his teams had won championships in six of his nine years as their boss on the field. When Scanlon first arrived in February, he tried to be friendly with the older man. Smiling, joking, moving in the loose style of the major leaguer. But Nakadai didn't respond. It was as if he'd built a chilly wall around himself, which few people could get past. Scanlon wasn't the only player who couldn't get close to the manager; the Japanese players were also kept at a distance. In the dugout or the clubhouse, Nakadai was always formal and correct. He spoke to the coaches. He spoke to the owners. But he spoke very little to the players. He let them know what he wanted: to win. But he did not ask about wives or children or restaurants. He didn't want to hear about personal problems. He demanded only that the players play the game the way it was supposed to be played, the way he *wanted* it to be played. Only Buddy Heater talked to the manager in a casual way, and that was out of the hearing of the others.

"I can't talk to him," Scanlon said. "I tried a few times. There's nothing there, nobody home. He's a technician, not a leader, certainly not a friend."

Heater sighed.

"Yeah. All he does is win."

"We have something to do with that."

Heater drained his beer and put the bottle on a table.

"You change your mind," he said, "you call me, okay?"

With that, Buddy Heater left and Scanlon was alone again, facing another night in another hotel. He started to open a beer and then stopped, thinking: Jesus Christ, I'll end up an alcoholic this way. So he went out, too, taking the empty elevator down to the lobby, out into the Japanese night. He liked walking here because he always felt safe. That was the first thing he'd noticed when he arrived in February with his agent. In the cities of America, he could never walk alone at night. Nobody there was safe, not even baseball stars. In Tokyo, for the first time since he was a boy, he could walk at night without a sense of menace.

But simple safety wasn't enough. Walking at night after a game, Scanlon only felt more isolated. He could not read the signs. He couldn't understand the headlines in the newspapers. He didn't know enough Japanese to be polite. He looked at pretty women and wished he could speak to them and couldn't think of a word to say. Even tonight, three months after arriving, he stopped outside a restaurant and realized that he could not even read the menu, could not order food, would not know how to pay.

Then, outside an appliance store, he saw a small crowd of people watching a row of television sets. He stood at the fringe of the crowd. The news was playing on all the sets, and then suddenly the afternoon's game was being reported. And there it was again: the Giants' batter slicing a line drive to left field, Scanlon loping in, hesitating, letting the ball drop, picking it up, firing to the cutoff man. The run scored. And there was Nakadai, out on the steps, his fury barely contained, waving at Scanlon to come in, pulling him out of the game, one of the young Japanese outfielders taking a glove out to play the position. And there was Scanlon, looking baffled, his hands on his hips, not quite understanding, and then, humiliated, walking back to the dugout. A close-up showed Scanlon scowling at Nakadai, then slamming his glove against the bench in rage. The newscaster continued speaking, his face grim. And there on the street, Scanlon eased away from the crowd, afraid that someone might recognize him.

He circled back toward the hotel, thinking about Nakadai. What could I tell him anyway? That I was afraid of hurting the shoulder again? That I misplayed the ball? That I thought Nakadai had a point and I was sorry? Hell, no. Besides, the guy just doesn't like me very much. Didn't like me from the day I showed up. Didn't even come to the fucking press conference at the airport. Scanlon talked to his agent a few weeks after he arrived, the agent back in Los Angeles, and the agent said that the manager's chilliness was probably simple: Nakadai didn't want Scanlon on the team. He had his outfielders set. He wanted a *pitcher*. "You gotta show him, man," the agent said. "You gotta prove to him that he needs you. Even if he doesn't."

Obviously, the agent knew that Scanlon would never again be the player he was in his mid-twenties. The broken shoulder four years before was the worst of it, but a year later there was the ruptured tendon in the left leg. For the past three seasons, there had been too many doctors, X rays, pills and pain. Even DH-ing for Texas had been a struggle. But going to Japan this year, he felt physically better than he had in years. And the money was more than he could get from any team in the States. The agent warned him that reports of his high salary could cause jealousy and dissension among the

Japanese players. "You just have to beat the crap out of the ball," the agent said. "That way nobody will complain."

But right from the start, Scanlon made some mistakes. In spring training in Kyushu, he reacted to the strenuous exercises the way so many other American players had: he resisted. The days were too long, the exercises too hard; he was afraid of reinjuring the shoulder or the leg; he asked to be excused and Nakadai insisted that he go on. "You will work out the pain," the manager said through his interpreter, ending the discussion. Every night, Scanlon fell into deep, exhausted sleep.

But then Scanlon made his second mistake. He gave an interview to a visiting reporter from *The New York Times* saying what he thought of the Japanese version of spring training. He told the truth and made some dumb jokes. The *Times* printed what he said. And then the Japanese sports papers picked up the story and Scanlon was marked as the latest candidate for the title of Ugly American. There was one every year in Japanese baseball. Perhaps he wasn't as bad as Joe Pepitone, the ex-Yankee who had been a public disgrace, but he was certainly inching down that path. For the first time, Buddy Heater took him aside to give him advice. Each team was allowed two American players on the roster and Heater was the other one.

"This is their country," Heater said. "They pay you with *their* money. So you play the game the way *they* want to play it. It's a little different from the way we play it. But it ain't *that* different. It's still baseball."

That time, back in the spring, Heater smiled and said: "Besides, you will get in the best shape of your life."

So Scanlon went through the grueling exercises and Buddy Heater tried to explain what he called the samurai way of playing baseball. Team spirit. Playing through pain. Dignity. Respect for the opponent. Sacrifice. Scanlon smiled; it sounded like a lecture from some Midwestern preacher. This was baseball and he had come to understand that baseball was not what he thought it was when his father handed him a bat and said, without words, play this game and I will love you. Love was no longer part of the equation. Baseball now was just another part of the entertainment business. You played for the team that paid you the most money. There was no loyalty, not to other players, or to the towns where you played, or to the owners or managers. And they felt no loyalty to you. You sold them your skills, the way an actor did to a movie studio, and box office was all that mattered. "Remember, kid," an old player told him once, "it doesn't matter how many seats there are in the ballpark. What matters is how many asses there are in the seats." You tried to channel your personal tension into performance and put asses in those seats. In exchange, they gave you money and when the season ended, everyone moved on. That was baseball. This year you were in New York, playing for the Yankees; next year it could be Milwaukee; the year after that, Japan.

"Baseball is baseball," Scanlon said wearily one night. "It doesn't matter where the fuck you play it." Buddy Heater disagreed. He suggested that Scanlon learn something about the history and traditions of baseball in Japan, learn about Sadaharu Oh, who had more home runs than Hank Aaron, or Shigeo Nagashima, one of the greatest natural hitters in the history of baseball, or Kazuhisa Inao, the "Iron Man" pitcher of the Nishitetsu Lions. "They got their heroes too, man," Buddy Heater said. "And these guys, every *one* of them coulda played in the States. They didn't, 'cause they were proud to play *here*. You gotta respect that."

But the names were only names and Scanlon couldn't find people who had seen the men play and didn't know how to ask for videos of them in their glory years. So he learned nothing. He did adjust to the grueling training exercises, and as Buddy predicted, he did start the season in great shape. After three weeks, he was hitting .379 and had 9 home runs. Nakadai said nothing. For one thing, Scanlon wasn't hitting well with men on base. Instead of placing a safe single that would score a run, he'd swing for the fences and usually strike out. Once, ordered to bunt to move a runner along, he looked astonished, as if saying: me, *bunt*? In another game, Scanlon went 0-for-4, leaving three runners on base, and Nakadai benched him for three days. "He says you are tired," the interpreter explained. "He says you need rest." Scanlon fumed, then sulked. Buddy Heater told him to relax. "Easy for you to say. *You*'re playing," Scanlon said. "And you're only hitting .235." Heater smiled: "Yeah, but I'm playing for the team and you're playing for yourself."

Scanlon thought about that for a day and then shrugged it off. Sure, I'm playing for myself. I can't even talk to these fucking guys, my so-called teammates. I can't talk to the manager. I'm alone. Except for Heater. And he's really one of *them*. Scanlon did get to play again, of course, and went on a tear, hitting home runs, batting for average. Then after one home run, he went into a slow, arrogant jog as he rounded the bases, the way so many players did back home. The next day he was benched again.

Remembering all of that now, walking through the hot Tokyo evening, Scanlon grew more angry. He remembered Buddy Heater reciting a Japanese saying: "The nail that sticks out gets hammered." Home run trots, interviews, complaints, displays of emotion: all were unacceptable to men of Nakadai's generation. And he realized that here he would always be a nail that stuck out.

3

He came back into the hotel around midnight. Buddy was sitting in the lobby, smoking a cigar and reading *Newsweek*.

"I want to talk to him," Scanlon said. "Now."

"Now?" Heater said. "Forget it. He's in bed."

"Wake him up."

"*You* wake him up."

Heater looked at his cigar.

"I think I will," Scanlon said.

Heater sighed. "If you insist, my man . . ."

Nakadai answered the door of the room on the fourth floor.

Heater bowed and said in Japanese that Mr. Scanlon would like to speak to his manager. Nakadai returned the bow, then grunted. He was wearing a short robe and sandals. His face was freshly shaved. He motioned for Scanlon and Buddy to come into the room. A tape of that day's game was playing on the television set and a pad of paper lay on the bed, covered with notes.

"I want to know why you have a bug up your ass about me," Scanlon said bluntly.

Buddy translated and Nakadai looked annoyed. He said a few words.

"He says he don't have a bug up his ass," Buddy explained. "Or words to that effect."

Nakadai used a remote control to stop the tape. One of his players had just been called out on strikes. It was the sixth inning. He made a note, and then, without looking at Scanlon, he started to talk quickly, precisely.

"What he says is that you are still a spoiled boy," Buddy explained. "He recognizes that you have talent. But talent is only 10 percent of the game. The rest is will and character. He didn't want you on the team, he says. But when the season started, he saw your talent. He was surprised you could still play as well as you could. He didn't expect that. But you probably always had talent and thought talent was enough. After a player is twenty-five, he says, work is more important than talent. And you don't work hard enough. You have a bad attitude. You showboat. You don't give a good example to his young players."

Scanlon said angrily that he worked hard through all of his career, but that he didn't think it was necessary to *show* how hard he worked. Heater translated. Nakadai smiled thinly and answered.

"He says that the sad thing is that you probably believe that."

"Who the hell does he think he is? He doesn't know *me*! He's never even had a talk with me."

Nakadai shook his head. He went to the bureau and poured a small drink of sake. He offered it to Scanlon, who paused for a beat.

"Take it," Heater said. "Have some manners, for Chrissakes."

Scanlon sipped the warm sake. Nakadai then gave Heater a drink and poured one for himself. He stared at Scanlon. And then spoke again.

"He says he's not paid to talk," Heater said. "He's not a psychiatrist. Or a politician. Or a television broadcaster. He's a baseball manager. He's paid to watch and to see, to think, and then to *act*. He sees you. He watches what you do, how you behave. When you refused to dive for the ball today, he understood. You were afraid to injure your shoulder again. And he sympathizes with you. . . . But he couldn't allow such an act of selfishness to go unpunished. It wasn't personal. It was what he is paid to do."

Scanlon's anger was ebbing now. The manager's words were like a cold shower. And most of them were true. Nakadai said a few more things and finished his drink. So did Heater.

"Now he's gotta return to his work," Buddy Heater said. "He's gotta finish studying today's game. He thanks you for coming to see him."

"Wait," Scanlon said. He felt a surge of drama filling the room. "He can't just dismiss me like that."

"Come on, man," Heater whispered. "Tomorrow's another day."

"No," Scanlon said. "There's something else going on. Underneath all this. Something he's not saying."

While Heater explained this to Nakadai, Scanlon took the old laminated photograph from his wallet. The picture of the scared boy and his ball-playing father. He thrust it at Nakadai, who took it gently from the American's hand.

"See that?" Scanlon said. "That's my father. He's dead now, but that's how long I've played baseball. Since way back *then*. I love baseball. I want to play baseball. I even want to play for Mr. Nakadai. Every day. Tell him that."

Nakadai studied the photograph, then looked at Scanlon with those hawk's eyes and handed it back to the American. He muttered a few more words.

"He said the photograph proves you loved your father. It don't prove you love baseball." A pause. "And Nakadai-san says it proves another thing: he loves baseball and you don't. That's the big difference between you two."

Scanlon looked as if he'd been slapped. The shower was very cold now and he could not make it warm. He lowered the hand that held the photograph. Then, very formally, he bowed to Nakadai, murmuring his thanks.

"He's right," he whispered to Heater.

"Hey, man . . ."

Scanlon felt empty now, and then suddenly the chill left him, and he began to feel warm again.

He said: "Tell him one final thing: I'm going home tomorrow. It's over for me, man. I'm packing it in."

"You *serious?*" Heater said.

"Yeah," Scanlon said. "Maybe for the first time in my life."

"I'll tell him," Heater said. "But you want to sleep on it?"

"No," Scanlon said. "He's right. I gotta go find something to love. It ain't baseball. Maybe it never was."

He bowed and went out, leaving Heater with Nakadai, and he walked down the hall. The sentence was over. The life sentence had been commuted. The bars were off all the windows. Near the elevator there was a small trash can. He dropped the old photograph into the can and stepped into the elevator, feeling light and young and free as he hurried to his room to pack.

The Magic Word

1

Every evening in the long silence before sleep, Masayuki traveled through space and time to the magical delta of Louisiana. He was eleven years old now, and had not seen Louisiana since he was eight. But when Masayuki closed his eyes, he was once again leaving the back door of the long, low white house where they lived and running through the fields of high, wet grass; once again, he smelled the sea odor of the bayous; once again, he heard the caw of strange birds soaring on the winds of the Gulf of Mexico. Up ahead was the dry land and the field where they played baseball. His friends were named Jesse and Carl and Willie John, and they were always there, in the place of magic.

So much of what he remembered of Louisiana was magic. Masayuki was five when he arrived. His father had come first, to manage the plant in the city nearby and to find the low white house for his wife and son. But when the boy moved into his huge, bright room and looked for the first time at American television, he was frightened. He spoke no English. Not a word. And understood nothing on television. When he met the American boys, fishing in the bayou, he tried to speak and only Japanese came out. The boys teased him and Masayuki cried and ran away. But each day, his loneliness drove him back and the boys stopped teasing him and spoke very slowly. And then one day, as if by magic, he was speaking English, quickly and fluently, great whole paragraphs of words flowing out of him. And Jesse and Carl and Willie John talked to him about everything—snakes and football and girls and insects—and changed his name to Max because they couldn't say Masayuki.

Baseball was subject to the same magic. The American boys were all bigger than he was and played with power and natural grace. The first time he played with them, he tried to field a ball and it smashed against his hand, stinging his whole arm, and caromed into the out-field for a hit. He dropped three other balls in that terrible game. And struck out each time he came to bat. But he kept coming back, kept trying, and then one day, the magic happened: every ball fell into his quick hands, every throw across the infield was fast and accurate. He could still not hit with power, but Willie John taught him how to bunt, and since he could run very fast, he could always bunt for a base hit. Jesse taught him how to get a jump on the pitch-er, and fall away when sliding into second to steal the base cleanly. Yes, he was still too small to hit with power, but if you could steal second, then a bunt was the same as a double. And it had all hap-pened like magic.

But that was a long time ago now, in another country. Now he would lie in his four-and-a-half tatami-mat room in the apartment in Tokyo and listen to his mother's shallow breathing in the next room and try to make Louisiana real. He wanted his dreams to take him there and thought that if he made the images absolutely real before sleep, he would dream through the night about those van-ished fields. The attempt to make a dream never worked. He dreamed instead of vicious dogs and black rivers. He dreamed of car crashes and serpents.

Once he woke up, screaming for his father. His mother rushed in and tried to console him. But when she was gone, he remembered the night his father died and how the American policeman came to the house, looking grave and sad. His Southern accent was too thick for his mother to understand, for she had learned only textbook English in high school. So Masayuki had to explain to her what had happened. There had been an automobile crash. "He was doing about ninety," the policeman said. "Appears he was doin' a little drinkin' . . ." His mother wailed and tore at her hair and fell thrash-

ing upon the couch and wailed again. But when she was finished
and there were no tears left, his father was still dead and the time in
Louisiana was over.

When he imagined the green fields, he never saw his father.

2

In the mornings now in Tokyo, his mother went to work but
Masayuki went nowhere. He didn't go to school anymore. From the
time when he first came back to Japan, the other boys had made fun
of him. They laughed at the way he sprinkled English words in his
sentences or groped for the correct word in Japanese. They teased
him because his handwriting was terrible and his *kanji* characters
danced like demented snakes. His mother moved him from one
school to another, three schools in all, and enlisted tutors to help
him, but the trouble only got worse. He had more and more fights
with older boys, the bullies of the schoolyard. And then he just
stopped going to class. Late one morning, he saw a television pro-
gram about the problem of the *kikoku shijo*, the children of overseas
businessmen who had returned to Japan. He realized he was one of
them. That's what he was: not a boy but a problem. And he retreated from the world.

He made his retreat into the world of *manga*, the great thick
comic books that were sold everywhere in Tokyo. He piled the
books high against the wall in his small room and spent his days
reading. He had always been able to draw and he started copying the
figures from the *manga*, filling the pages of his unused composition
books. Every week, with money from his allowance, he bought
Shonen Jump and *Shonen Champion* and he discovered a store
where he could trade for old *manga*. The only book he never traded
was *Magic Man*.

Magic Man was about a young orphan boy with a crippled leg
who had learned a magic word from an old wizard. The magic word
was, of course, a secret; it had to be, because it transformed the boy

into Magic Man, rippling with muscles, dashing and handsome in a scarlet costume, his face masked, a cape swirling, possessor of a magic sword. With the sword, Magic Man could slay his enemies. He could defend the weak and the innocent. With his sword, he could travel great distances by simply pointing the sword into the sky and speaking the name of the destination. Masayuki loved Magic Man. If he were Magic Man, he would point his sword across great oceans to the green fields of Louisiana.

"This is for you," his mother said when she came home from work one evening. She handed him a large wrapped package. He held it for a long moment. He hadn't even talked to her for several weeks, closing up tightly inside of himself. And here she was, offering him a gift. Slowly, he removed the wrapping. Inside the package was a book about drawing *manga*, a pad of clean white paper, some pens and brushes and ink. "You draw so well," she said. "Maybe you can become a cartoonist." Masayuki started to cry and when his mother hugged him and said she only wanted him to be happy, he told her that he was happy, the ink and paper and brushes were beautiful. But he felt terrible too. He said: "You have spent a lot of money on these."

"I want you to go back to school," she whispered softly. "Even writers of *manga* must go to school."

So that was it: she had a plan. And perhaps she was right. He began to study the book about drawing *manga*, reading about famous cartoonists, men named Nakazawa and Matsumoto and Tezuka. And one night, while his mother worked late, he saw a television story about one of the cartoonists; he was sitting on a beach in Hawaii, surrounded by pretty women, driving a large car, writing *manga*. And he thought for the first time: maybe it's possible, maybe I really can be a cartoonist. He thought: I could buy a large white house. He thought: my mother could stop working. He thought: I could go back to Louisiana and see Jesse and Carl and Willie John.

Masayuki began to draw all day long. Copying at first from all the comics, but then almost always drawing Magic Man. His efforts never pleased him. For one thing, he couldn't get the bodies of the women right. When he tried ink and brush, his lines were thick and clumsy, without the sinuous quality of the originals, where the line was thin here and thick there. But he kept doing it, hoping that the magic would happen to him again, as it did when he was learning baseball and English. His mother continued to bring him supplies and he started calling his room his "studio."

Soon he'd mastered the features of Magic Man and could draw his face without copying. The bodies of his women still looked like men but their faces were more elegant. His line was still too thick. But he was getting better. He was sure of that. He began to sign his Magic Man drawings, imitating the signature of the artist, whose name was Babe Sasaki. And in the comics store, he talked to the owner and some of the regular customers about this great man.

"Babe Sasaki?" one teenaged customer said. "I never heard of him."

The owner smiled and said, "Oh, yes, Sasaki. Poor man. Well, he had his day. But now . . ."

He shrugged Sasaki away, the way a stranger might shrug off the report of an auto accident that happened to someone else. Masayuki noticed too that the references to Sasaki in the *manga* fan magazines were not frequent and almost never flattering. Magic Man was always dismissed as a leftover from the distant past. This made the boy angry and defensive. To Masayuki, Magic Man was a new comic book, a new hero; *he* hadn't been reading it for twenty-five years. And besides, who could deny that Babe Sasaki was one of the old masters of Japanese cartooning? It said so in the books about *manga*. Sasaki was part of the generation of men who started drawing comics after the war. His great period was in the 1950s, one article said, when Japan was still weak, still rebuilding and boys needed images of power. But *manga* had changed in the 1960s and were still changing. They were more sophisticated now, more complicated, at once more realistic and more imaginative . . .

Masayuki read these words, and heard the remarks in the comics store, but didn't truly understand. To him, it was all much simpler: Magic Man was the greatest *manga* in the world and therefore Babe Sasaki was the greatest artist.

And one afternoon, brooding upon the magic word that was never spoken in Magic Man, the word that transformed an orphan into a superhero, and angry at the unflattering words he'd heard spoken about Babe Sasaki, he wrote the great cartoonist a letter.

3

His mother was at work when the postman came to the door with a letter for Mr. Masayuki Takeuchi. The boy thanked the postman and looked at the letter and his heart started pounding. On the envelope, in beautiful type, were the words "Sasaki Productions." Inside was a letter, with the address across the top, and a pale gray image of Magic Man filling the whole page. The note was written over that image, in handsome, manly calligraphy.

Dear Masayuki, the letter said,

Thank you for your kind words about my work. And good luck in your own career as an aspiring cartoonist. If you would like to visit my studio some day, I am always there at 10 A.M.

It was signed by Babe Sasaki.

The boy glanced at his watch. It was already noon. Too late to visit the great man today. But he read the letter again, and then again, read it a dozen times, held it like some precious message from another world. Held it, in fact, like something imbued with the power of magic.

All that day, he worked on his drawings of Magic Man, not even pausing to eat the lunch his mother had left for him. And he kept going back to the letter, as if to assure himself that it was real. The address was in a district named Yamabuki-cho. He didn't know where that was. He would have to ask his mother how to get there on the subway. And it could be dangerous too: a policeman might see him, ask him why he wasn't in school, arrest him. But he had conceived a new dream. He would bring his drawings to Babe Sasaki and the great man would look at them and offer him a job. He could do whatever was necessary: clean up the office, wash brushes, deliver cartoons, run errands, make tea, fetch lunch. It didn't matter to Masayuki. Tomorrow he would begin his career. He would never have to go to school. He would become the youngest cartoonist in the history of Japan.

And there was something more important. He would ask Babe Sasaki for the secret that nobody else in Japan had ever learned: the magic word.

4

The next morning, with his drawings in a large envelope, he started for the studio of Babe Sasaki. According to the subway map his mother kept in the kitchen, he had to take the Tozai line to Iidabashi Station, then change to the Yurakucho line and get off at Edogawabashi station. But along the way, jammed in among adults on the crowded morning train, Masayuki began to feel a growing panic. He had never been on these trains alone. He'd never been to this district of Tokyo. He imagined Babe Sasaki working among great gleaming towers, the buildings of some future city. The studio would be vast, filled with a lifetime of work and everything that came with great fame. He was a boy from nowhere, one of the *kikoku shijo*, a boy without father or friends or money or school or job. Why would anyone as famous as Babe Sasaki waste time with him?

When he emerged at last from the subway in Yamabuki-cho, he wanted to turn around and go home. The area teemed with people and cars and strange faces. He asked one man for directions and was ignored. The panic swelled. Then he saw a policeman turning a corner and he retreated into the dark doorway of a restaurant. His stomach tightened. The policeman walked by without seeing him and Masayuki took a deep breath, and imagined himself as Magic Man. He would raise the sword, point it, speak the name of his destination, and would be transported there. All he needed was the magic word. And to discover the magic word, he must go on. He must meet Babe Sasaki. He must. Then a van pulled up and a man jumped out and began unloading cases of soda. He asked directions. The man gave him directions far more detailed than any map.

He passed the Teiken Gym, which he had seen on television in a story about boxers. Its doors were closed. He passed a school with mean-looking kids lounging outside, smoking cigarettes. He passed shuttered restaurants and small shops. And then, up ahead, he saw the building.

It rose twelve stories above the street and it did not gleam. The walls were glazed with dirt. A few windows were blocked out with cloth. A dirty white banner flapped in the breeze, offering offices for rent. Masayuki went into the dark empty lobby. There was a directory on the wall, with the names of companies made of small plastic letters stuck into felt. He discovered that he was in the right building; Sasaki Productions was on the sixth floor. There was one problem: an "out of order" sign was pasted on the doors of the lone elevator. Another sign, with an arrow, said: "Please use stairs."

Masayuki climbed the stairs, stopping after three flights for breath, then trudging on. At each landing, the door was marked with a number. Above him, twelve stories above the ground, he could see daylight and hear the sound of a creaking door.

At last he reached the sixth floor. He pushed open the heavy door and found himself in a long empty corridor. Fluorescent lights threw a pale blue wash over the walls. Most of the offices were closed. And at the far end, he saw lights behind a glass-paneled door. He walked slowly to the door. A sign said Sasaki Productions.

He knocked.

No answer.

He knocked again, gently, afraid that the great man might be working on some immense and complicated drawing of Magic Man. Again there was no answer. He tried the handle and the door opened.

Before him lay a great dark cave. On one wall, bound volumes of Magic Man *manga* filled all the shelves, and there were piles of loose copies on the floor, and still others piled on desks and drawing tables. Most were covered with dust. From the ceiling hung Magic Man dolls, Magic Man cups, plastic Magic Man swords, empty Magic Man costumes, all moving slightly from strings, everything embossed with the character's image, all souvenirs from a time when this was the most popular *manga* in Japan. A window looked out over Tokyo, but the glass was almost opaque from grime. The space was broken up by partitions into tiny cubbyholes, in each of which was an unused drawing table, a small taboret beside it, trays for pens, tacks, tape. All were covered with copies of old *manga*, or picture magazines, or file folders from which photographs spilled like old memories.

And in a far corner, her head down on a drawing table, the light burning above her, was a young woman. She was asleep. Masayuki walked over quietly, afraid to wake her. On the table was a Magic Man page. One panel remained drawn only in pencil. Beside her, there was an open bottle of ink. In her right hand, a brush, the ink already hardened on its bristles.

Masayuki backed away, bumped into an empty table, knocked down a large T square. The young woman came suddenly awake, her eyes wide.

"Who are you?" she said. "What are you doing here? What do you want?"

"I— I—"

She rubbed her eyes, looking more irritated than afraid. She wasn't pretty but she looked at him in a direct way that made her look grown-up and capable.

"Well?"

He fumbled in his envelope, found the letter. "I got a letter from Babe Sasaki and—"

"Oh, poor boy," she said. She was fully awake now and looked at the page and then at her watch. She got up and hurried to a sink and started washing the brush. She was tall, wearing slacks that were wrinkled and linty. "They're form letters. Some secretarial service answers them. He doesn't even read them." She paused. "I got one of his letters once too," she said in a voice that was gray with sadness. "I came over here too. I guess you want to be a cartoonist."

"Yes."

"And you brought drawings to show him?"

"Yes."

"Let me see."

She went back to the drawing table and dipped the brush in the ink, thinned it slightly by marking a scrap paper beside her, then started inking the penciled panels. She was very fast. Her line was thick and thin, her blacks juicy and rich. The woman in the panel was full-bodied and sexy and Magic Man came right off the page. Masayuki slipped his drawings out of the envelope, then pushed them back inside.

"Take them out again," she said, not looking up. He'd never before seen such concentration. "I'll be finished soon. Put them on that drawing table near the sink."

He laid them out on the table.

"Why aren't you in school?" she said, without turning her head. Her concentration seemed total.

"I don't go to school," the boy said.

"You have to go to school."

"I don't like it," he said quietly. "Besides, I was told Mr. Sasaki didn't go to school, because of the war, and—"

She looked up, her eyes sad.

"Yes," she said, with a hardness in her voice. "And look at what has become of him."

With some heat, he came to Sasaki's defense. "Look what he's done, look at all those books on the shelves, look how long he's lasted—"

She sighed. "Sasaki hasn't done a drawing in twenty years. I've done the book for three years. Before me there were others, many others."

She gazed out at the bright morning. And then the door slammed, and a small, balding old man lurched into the room. His skin made him look like a yellow prune. He had a cigarette jammed into his mouth, and when he bumped against one of the drawing tables Masayuki understood two things: this was Mr. Sasaki and he was drunk.

"Where is it?" he shouted. "Where's the story?"

"I'm on the last page," the young woman said drily.

"The last page?" he screamed, dropping the cigarette on the floor and mashing it out with his foot. "It's supposed to be finished, all thirty pages. I have a deadline in twenty minutes! Don't you know anything about deadlines?"

He paused and looked at Masayuki.

"Who the hell are you?" he said.

The boy stammered. "My n – name is, M – Masayuki," he blurted. "You said in your letter I could visit—"

He shook his head, opened a cabinet, took out a bottle of whiskey and poured a drink into a dirty glass.

"Are these your drawings?"

"Yes, sir.

The old man looked at them, his face contorted with rage, and then swept them violently off the table to the floor.

"Shit! All shit!"

The young woman stood up abruptly. "Sasaki-*san*! Stop it! He's a nice boy! You asked him to come here. . . ."

Sasaki shouted: "Sit down, woman! I have a deadline!"

He was planted between Masayuki and the door, and when the boy looked at him, Sasaki's figure was blurred from tears.

"What do you want?" the old man said. His eyes were full of rage. "What do you *want* from me?"

For Masayuki, the room was reeling now, the walls moving in and out. Masayuki could only whisper: "The magic word . . ."

And then Sasaki started to laugh.

"The magic word? You want the magic word? I *see*." He sipped from the dirty whiskey glass, slammed it on a littered table, then gazed in an unsteady way at all the Magic Man souvenirs. "You want the word that makes you big and powerful? The word that makes you able to defend the weak and fly to the four corners of the world?

"Yes," Masayuki whispered.

"I'll tell you the magic word, you little idiot! The magic word is . . . *money*! You got that? *Money*! Now pick up these crappy scrawlings of yours and get out of here!"

Masayuki reeled away, a high-pitched singing noise in his head. He bumped roughly against drawing tables, a desk, a chair, gasping for breath. He jerked open the door, seeing nothing through his tears, a hurt animal sound coming from his throat. He pulled on door after door, all of them locked, trying to find his way out, and then found the heavy door to the hall. Downstairs was the street and the walk back to the subway and the long ride home and his mother's disappointed face and the useless inks and brushes in his room. Downstairs lay all the terrors of the world.

He began to climb toward the light. He suddenly felt strong, his lungs powerful, his legs carrying him up the steps, past 7 and then 8, past 9 and 10 and 11, finally reaching 12. A rusted door hung loosely on its hinges. Through the rectangle of its frame, he could see clouds and birds and patches of blue sky, as neat as a scene in a panel of *manga*. He stepped out on the roof and found himself high above the world.

Then he saw them in the clouds, Jesse and Carl and Willie John. They were calling to him from the green fields. They had a ball and a bat and new gloves. Come on, Max, they said, drop a bunt down the third base line. He could smell the bayous. He could see strange birds. He moved forward to the edge of the roof. He could hear the rustle of the tall grass and feel the Gulf wind. And then he moved to the edge, raised his imaginary sword, whispered his own secret word, and stepped forward, to fly all the way to Louisiana.

It's Only Rock 'n' Roll

1

That year, Valentine was the hottest singer in the music business. She sold more albums than anyone else on earth. Her singles received more airplay on the radio stations of the world and her erotic videos played every hour on the many versions of MTV. Her steamy posters were tacked, glued or taped to the walls of uncountable rooms, from college dormitories to the tenements of the poor. Hundreds of thousands of young girls began wearing their hair the way she did, straight back, hanging past her shoulder blades. Even the girls who were not blondes. *Valentine . . .* It was impossible that summer to go anywhere without hearing her strong, powerful voice, fierce and passionate on the hard-driving tunes, lyrical on the ballads, its natural sweetness tempered by a hoarse rock 'n' roll burr. You heard the voice on jukeboxes. You heard it from huge radios played by teenagers. It came booming from giant television sets pitched high above bars. *Valentine,* they all said. *Valentine . . .*

"But what I want to know," she said one night to her friend Cynthia, who was back home in Gainesville, "is how come with all of this I'm not happy?"

Cynthia just laughed. So, in a dark way, did Valentine. "Jesus Christ," she said, echoing the storylines of ten thousand cheap celebrity interviews, "it's lonely at the top." She laughed too. But it really wasn't funny.

2

There were almost five thousand fans waiting for Valentine when she arrived at the airport in Narita on the last stop of her World Tour. The security people were near panic, afraid of snake dances or political demonstrations or even terrorists. But after a while, even the most suspicious policeman seemed to understand that this was *Valentine*. And Valentine was different. The fans, alas, saw almost nothing of her. Direct from passport control, she and the band were ushered into a private lounge where the press corps lay in wait. There were about two hundred of them: reporters and photographers and TV crews, with female translators asking the questions for the male reporters, the women reporters asking their own questions, and almost everybody smoking. She was asked some of the usual questions: How did she like Japan? And did she eat Japanese food in the States? And where did she get the idea for the song "I'm the Difference"? Kenny, the bass player, and her lover since the third day of the road trip, answered one question by saying: "I've always had a yen to go to Japan." The guys from the band laughed. Valentine had heard the joke on the plane and glanced at her watch.

Then a tall, slender Japanese man stood up. He was dressed more formally than the others, in suit and tie, and was wearing steel-rimmed glasses. In his left hand, he held a notebook on top of a tape recorder and gestured with the pen in his right hand.

"Miss Valentine," he said in English, "with all of your success, are you happy?"

She paused, then waved away the gathering cigarette smoke of the other reporters.

"I don't know," she said at last, almost whispering. Kenny glanced at her uneasily. "I just don't know ..."

She thought about the question all the way into Tokyo in the limousine, while Kenny brooded beside her. It was another one of those endless dumbhead questions that are asked and answered in fan magazines or supermarket tabloids. She remembered Cynthia, and how they laughed at *It's lonely at the top* . . . But there was something about the man who asked it. The tone of his voice. His stance. Maybe he wasn't just asking a question, she thought. Maybe he really wanted to know. Maybe (and this seemed most unlikely of all) he *cared*.

"What's the matter?" Kenny asked after a while.

"Nothing," she said, staring out the window. Some Japanese fans passed them in the next lane, waving frantically and holding up albums, and she waved back.

"Don't give me that," he said. He was from West Texas, tall and lean as gristle. "You got somethin' on ya mind."

"Just jet lagged," she lied.

He looked at her and didn't believe her.

"It was that guy, right?" he said. "The dude asked you was you happy."

She looked at him, shook her head, turned away.

"Give me a break," she said in a cynical way and closed her eyes.

In the suite at the New Otani, there were flowers and baskets of fruit and great mounds of telegrams and a bowl of M&Ms, because some magazine article had said that Valentine loved M&Ms. The promoter was there, smiling and gracious. The manager of the hotel showed up too, flanked by three members of his staff, and said that he would be available for anything she needed. That made the drummer laugh. Kenny popped open a bottle of iced champagne and poured four bubbling inches into a water glass. Finally Valentine thanked everybody and announced she had to sleep. The suite emptied, except for Kenny. She took him by the hand into the bedroom. An astronaut had told her once, at some forgotten party, that the only cure for jet lag was sex. And if an astronaut didn't know, who did? So she closed the blinds and slipped into bed and soon Kenny was beside her, smelling like sour apples. He made love to her angrily, almost savagely, without saying a word. She then rolled onto her side and went immediately to sleep.

When she woke up, Tokyo was dark and Kenny was gone. On the bar in the living room, she found two empty champagne bottles and one half-eaten apple. *Oh, you dumb fucking cowboy*, she thought, dropping one bottle in a wastebasket before going to the shower. She dressed in plain clothes, jeans and work shirt, the trademark blonde hair shoved up into a cap. She put on sunglasses, slipped the key into her pocket and went down to the lobby. Kenny must be there, in one of the bars, drinking with the band. The usual bullshit of the road, all of them trying to pick up groupies. A regular asshole contest.

When she came out of the elevator into the vast lobby, she saw the Japanese man sitting on a couch. The man who had asked the question at the press conference. He stood up and came forward. A security man suddenly appeared from the side, moving between them, but Valentine waved him away. He retreated in a surly way, as suspicious of Valentine as he was of the man.

"Miss Valentine," the man said, "please forgive me. I'm afraid I embarrassed you with my silly question."

She smiled at his formality and said, "I'm sorry I didn't give you much of an answer."

He told her his name was Teru and he was a writer and he had worked in Los Angeles for a few years and in London before that. He wasn't a music writer. He wrote about cultural phenomena. "Am I a phenomena?" she said, smiling. And he said no, she was a phenomenon, singular not plural, absolutely unique. "You must be aware of it," he said. "You are known everywhere."

She thought it would sound stupid for a phenomenon to ask him if he'd seen her bass player. So she smiled and shook his hand.

"I'm going to be locked up here in this hotel for four days," she said. "Like a goddamned prisoner. So can I ask you a favor? Could you take me for a walk outside, out there in Tokyo?"

Teru bowed slightly. "Of course."

3

She told the security man to stay put and then she and Teru walked out of the hotel into the night air. The streets were empty, but lights still burned in office buildings. They walked a few blocks and then started across a small bridge with water shimmering below. "A river in Tokyo!" she said. "God, I love rivers, I grew up near a river. I always thought they'd take me away to the sea, to freedom . . ."

Teru smiled: "But it's not a river, it's a moat. To protect the emperor."

She asked a hundred questions about the emperor and his wife and Japanese history and he answered in his smooth English and seemed to laugh in the right places. They passed through a brightly lit district of bars and restaurants and she kept repeating its name as if it were some amusing mantra: "Akasaka, Akasaka, Akasaka, . . ." But the faces inside were all young. Valentine didn't want to risk being recognized so they walked for many blocks on the warm starless summer night. The rhythm was established: she asked dozens of questions and he answered them cleanly and crisply and with what she sensed was great pride. He was born here, in Tokyo; it was his city, and he knew it the way she had known Gainesville, Florida, when she was a small girl with braces on her teeth, riding a bicycle on summer afternoons. They walked on under the Tokyo street-lights. The shops were all closed, and though the streets were almost empty (for it was after midnight now), she felt no sense of menace. Then up ahead she saw the dark glade of the Nogi Shrine. He told her its name.

"I want to see it," she said, moving ahead of him into the winding paths of the gardens. He tried to explain the differences between Shinto and Buddhism but she seemed unable to focus on the distinctions. "What does the name mean?" she said. "What's a Nogi?" He told her about Nogi Maresuke, who was the commander of the Third Army during the war with the Russians in 1905 and how he lost sixty thousand troops taking Port Arthur. He had lived here, near his troops, in that small clapboard house he showed her through the trees beside the shrine. He kept a white horse in the stable, a horse given to him by the Russian commander after the great battle, and here in this house, when the Emperor Meiji died, Nogi and his wife committed ritual suicide.

"But *why?*" she said, her eyes wide.

"Because that was the way it was done in those days," he said, and shrugged. She liked that. Quick and simple, like a good song lyric. He didn't need to deliver an elaborate lecture on the history of Japan. Not to her. Not this late at night in a dark glade. She smiled to herself at one point, wondering if the band would commit ritual suicide if *she* died, then thought, shit, they're probably committing ritual suicide right now. Teru started back to the street and suggested that they take a taxi to the hotel.

"No, no, please," she said. "If you have the time and legs, let's just walk. I spend all my time in airplanes and limousines and hotels. I don't know one town from another. But this is my first time here. I want to . . . feel it."

So they walked and walked, their path describing a great wide rectangle. Finally they passed the old Sanno Hotel, where (he explained to her) the Americans had established the Officers Club during the years of the Occupation. He smiled in an ironical way: "My father would not walk on this street for the rest of his life. That hotel was the symbol of his defeat and his humiliation." She said: "What about you?" Teru shrugged and said, "To me it means almost nothing." And then they were back to Akasaka and Teru led her into a side street and finally, into a small coffee shop. Jazz was playing on the sound system. A few older men sat alone, smoking cigarettes and reading newspapers.

"It's Monk," he said, after ordering coffee. "Do you like him?"

"Monk?" she said.

So Teru explained to her about Thelonious Monk and Charlie Parker, Dizzy Gillespie and Max Roach. She knew nothing about them. To her, the distant past was the year the Beatles came to

America. They ordered more coffee, and talked, and had little cakes, and talked some more, and then finally he looked at his watch and told her it was almost three in the morning.

"You must be having a busy day," he said. "The promoters surely have arranged a full schedule, publicity, then the concert."

"If it's too busy," she said, "I'll do what my man Nogi did."

"That would break too many hearts," he said. "At any rate, if we don't return soon, the security men will think you've been kidnapped."

He called for the check.

"What about you?" she said. "Won't your wife be worried?"

"I have no wife," he said, his face suddenly blank.

She stared at him, waiting, knowing he would explain. And he did.

"She died," he said, and then stared into the coffee and for the first time took out a package of cigarettes. "She was twenty-four years old, younger than you." He lit a cigarette with a small lighter, took a drag, his face a stoic mask. "She was driving to meet me in the country and a drunken man crashed into her."

She reached across the table and squeezed his hand.

4

He came to the concert that night, standing below the stage with the other reporters. Valentine noticed him during one of her ballads. His face was serious, he scribbled notes. They made no eye contact. At several moments, she seemed annoyed, as Kenny played erratically, now hammering hard power chords, now falling a hair behind the beat; the drummer had to work hard to maintain the beat. The fans didn't notice but Valentine did. Before the end of the concert, a roadie muscled his way into the press area and commanded Teru to follow him backstage.

By the time he made his way into the dressing room area, a party was under way. There was a packed bar and a table groaning with food and hostesses dressed in kimono. The executives of the record company were there too, and a few chosen reporters and some shy young girls with passes from the band. Teru kept taking notes. The band members started emerging from their dressing rooms and rushed to the crowded bar, shaking hands, smiling, smoking cigarettes, hugging the girls with the passes. Kenny was last to come out. His eyes were red.

Then a security man approached Teru and led him down a ramp to a line of waiting limousines. He stopped at the second car and held the door open.

"Miss Valentine will be here in five minutes," the man said in an Osaka accent. Teru climbed inside and the door thumped behind him. A chauffeur sat in silence beyond a glass divider. Then Teru heard commotion behind him, footfalls, shouts. And then the door opened and Valentine was there.

"You're here," she said. "Thank God."

And hugged him.

They went to the suite at the New Otani. She ordered dinner from room service and then told the operator to cut off all calls. They talked until two in the morning and then they went to bed.

"I want someone to make me happy," she whispered, almost desperately. "I want you to try."

They woke after dawn to a pounding on the door. Teru watched her go to the living room, her pink-nippled breasts bobbing, her ass smooth and white. She stopped at the door, where a special chain had been draped to protect her from zealous fans.

"Kenny," she shouted, "for Chrissakes, *go away!*"

Kenny's voice came from the other side of the door but Teru couldn't make out the words. He did understand the fury. And the drunkenness.

"I don't want to see you," she said. "I've got someone *here!*"

That made him crazier. He started pounding and kicking at the door and then she was back in the bedroom, still naked, and picked up the telephone and asked for security. "Please don't have him arrested," she said. "He's just drunk."

She hung up, and sat at the edge of the bed, staring at nothing. Teru thought her skin was as pale as snow.

"Shit," she said. "It always turns to shit."

Teru reached for the long blonde hair and the long snowy body.

5

Kenny didn't play at the second show. A Japanese bass player took his place, a student of Valentine's records; he performed carefully and solidly but without passion. Kenny took a room at another hotel and when Teru asked about him, Valentine said that he'd be all right.

"He'll get drunk for three days," she said, "and he'll be on the plane when we go home."

She laughed, and added: "It's only rock 'n' roll."

They made love for hours that night, and when they woke, they wandered again through Tokyo, Valentine dressed now like a businesswoman, Teru in a sport shirt. Nobody noticed them, as long as her trademark hair was out of sight. He brought her flowers. He brought her two CDs by Thelonious Monk and they listened to them over and over again on a portable player, while Teru explained her country's music to her. On the third day, she wore a black wig and that made Teru laugh. But that night, after the final concert and after they'd made love, she began to cry.

"I don't want to go home," she said. "I want to stay here. I mean it, Teru. No bullshit. We could buy a house in the mountains or out at the ocean. No telephone, no television." Her voice quickened, the words tumbling out now. "You can teach me Japanese. I'll give up the road, make a record once a year. Right *here*. I mean, the studios are great, they tell me, and the musicians—"

And then she stopped. The brief moment of hope died. Teru touched her face.

"Come," he said. "We'll go for another walk."

They slipped out through a side door. Rain was falling steadily on Tokyo and the streets were darker. They had no umbrella. Teru held her tightly. "Maybe you could come to the States with me," she said. He told her that would be impossible. "My work is here," he said quietly. "But perhaps . . . ah, who knows?" His voice trailed off. They walked for many blocks, soaked with rain. The wheels of passing cars made the sound of tearing silk. They did not notice the slow-moving taxi, a block behind them. She stopped when they reached the Nogi Shrine.

"What happened to the horse?" she said.

"The horse?"

"The white horse," she said. "The one the Russian commander gave to Nogi."

"I don't really know," he said.

"I hope they sent him home," she said.

"Maybe he was happy here," Teru said.

"I hope he was happy somewhere," she said.

And then he was upon them: Kenny, drunk and dirty and soaked with rain, his long hair plastered to his skull. Teru turned, saw the door of the taxi hanging open. And the big American coming in a hard rage. He threw a punch.

"You Jap son of a bitch!"

Teru slipped to the side, and Kenny went past him and fell hard. He rolled, cursed, still enraged, and started to get up. A door slammed; the taxi drove off.

Valentine screamed: "Kenny, what are you *doing*? Get out of here, get the fuck out of here!"

"Shut up, bitch."

He stood up, a foot taller than Teru.

"You want this phony blonde bitch," he snarled, "you better fight me for her!"

"I hate fighting," Teru said. "But I hate drunks more."

Kenny came in a rush, and Teru moved imperceptibly and drove a fist to his stomach, making a whooshing sound. Kenny bent over.

Then Valentine stepped between them and screamed: "Don't, please don't, don't fight, please—"

But it was too late. Kenny grabbed Teru, hurled him out into the rain-slick street and went after him. He wound up another punch and missed and then another and knocked Teru down. He started to stomp the smaller man but Valentine grabbed him. He grabbed her with both hands and slammed her to the pavement.

"You goddamn bitch!" Kenny screamed. "Stay there, baby, 'cause I'm gonna stomp your ass too."

But when he turned, Teru was up, his jacket off now, and his face altered. His eyes were sharply focused, his body crouched, his hands held in the way of a fighter.

By the time he was finished, Kenny lay in a broken pile. Teru stood in the rain, his hands at his side, gasping for breath. From his left eyebrow, a thin rill of blood turned pink in the rain. He turned and saw Valentine sitting on the edge of the sidewalk. Her head was on her knees, her body heaving with sobs while a stream of rainwater rushed downhill beneath her. "Go away," she said. "Go away." He looked at her for a long time. Then a taxi came along slowly and stopped. Teru bowed formally to Valentine and she looked at him and shook her head. "It's lonely at the fucking top," she said, and got into the taxi. He watched her go.

"Sayonara," he whispered.

He saw Kenny stirring, filthy with dirt and blood. He picked up his soaked jacket and walked for blocks until he found another taxi. The driver was annoyed at how wet Teru was and insisted that he sit on newspapers. Then Teru gave directions to his apartment and sat back, wet and cold and exhausted. His body hurt. His hands were raw. He stanched the cut over his eye with a handkerchief. Then the taxi turned into that street where his father would never walk, and as the driver passed the old Sanno Hotel, Teru thought about a beautiful horse, as white as snow, lost and bewildered and alone, in the wrong country.

Missing in Action

It was snowing gently when Thompson left the theater in Asakusa. He had spent the late afternoon in the close fish-smelling warmth of the *yose*, listening to a *rakugo* comedian tell hilarious stories about samurai without underwear. When he wasn't laughing, Thompson dutifully entered the outlines of these stories into a notebook. Later, he would type the stories into his laptop and much later, after he had returned to the United States, he would analyze them and write about them and thus produce still another book in the expanding shelf of unread books by Americans about Japanese popular culture. He thought: *It's a silly way to make a living but no sillier than many others. I could have been a cop. Or a general. Or a goddamned politician. But a professor . . . I start out to be a novelist, to live a great, gaudy romantic life like Hemingway, that miserable prick, and I end up . . . what? A goddamned professor.*

He stood for a moment with the snow melting in his hair, then lit a cigarette, inhaling deeply. The streets were crowded, with people hurrying home or slipping into the many restaurants. Young men snatched at the late editions of the sporting papers. Filipino girls with thick makeup hurried into bars for a night of peddling romance. He saw a middle-aged man in a business suit, the epitome of modern rationalism, pause to have his fortune told. On such wintry evenings, Thompson loved Tokyo. The snow silenced the city and softened its harsh edges and made all the women look beautiful. At the same time, he felt oddly isolated by the falling snow and that isolation reminded him of Japan when he'd first seen it, long ago, when he was

young and spoke no Japanese and knew no history. *Make me dumb
again, he thought. Let me know nothing and experience everything.*

He wandered down the street and into a pachinko parlor. The
sound of dropping coins and balls was as oddly soothing as the
silence of the falling snow. For Thompson, pachinko was like baseball, with its own rules, traditions, private rhythms. You either got it
or you didn't, and those who didn't usually dismissed it as boring;
they never seemed capable of surrendering to its spirit of contem-
plation. Thompson got it (or thought he did) and played for more
than an hour, losing himself in the game, entering after the first ten
minutes an almost Zen-like zone of psychological emptiness. He did
not think. He did not see. He vanished into the geometries of the
game.

Then a truck backfired outside, breaking the spell.

And when Thompson looked up, he saw Hearns.

He was two aisles away, his face visible in a three-quarter view
between the machines. He was deep into pachinko, his body
hunched and coiled.

Thompson's heart tripped. Then his pulse quickened.

Sergeant Hearns.

Can't fucking believe it.

Hearns! You rat bastard.

He was heavier and wore a graying beard now, and his hair was
thinner. But it was Hearns all right.

You son of a bitch.

Thompson paused, hearing the nickled clicking of pachinko
balls, the clattering of coins, and suddenly Vietnam was in the long,
crowded room: ghostly helicopters rising from open fields, pale
images of napalm scudding in the foothills outside Bong Son,
shredded bodies rotting in the yards of Buddhist monasteries,
gravestones carrying French names sinking into the mud outside Da
Nang. He looked again at Hearns and he was no longer in this pachinko parlor. He was in the compound in Pleiku on the night they
were mortared and Sergeant Hearns sat there staring into the dark-

ness, locked in an arctic silence. Once more, Thompson was on patrol that day, when they came into the hamlet without a name and Hearns ordered them to kill everybody, including the women and the children and the old men, and Thompson flat-out fucking refused, sick of the killing and the half-assed graves, and then four others made their separate refusals and Hearns in a cold rage knew that if he killed the Vietnamese he would have to kill the Americans too. So he killed nobody. But the sergeant didn't forget. After that day, Thompson was his enemy. More so than the Vietcong.

For months, the sergeant tried to get Thompson killed. He made him the point man on all patrols, out front as the platoon plunged into jungles. The point man was always the first to step on the mines. The point man was the one who took the first raking of machine gun fire. Usually, the men in the platoon took turns at the job, realizing that death in combat was a kind of lottery. But as sergeant, Hearns could make the assignments. Once Thompson's friend Barker came to him at night and said: "You'll have to kill this motherfucker before he kills you." Thompson laughed. A month later, after almost being killed four different times, Thompson was no longer laughing. He went to Hearns and told him: "If you don't take me off point, I'm gonna kill you."

Hearns laughed. "Just try, boy."

But he never had to try.

All of that came surging back in this pachinko parlor in Tokyo on a day peaceful with snow. *You prick*, he thought. *You cold-assed prick.* And he remembered the night when the platoon went out in a rubberized boat, doing recon on some forlorn river that meandered sluggishly through a jungle valley. They wedged the boat under some trees along the bank of the river, and Hearns ordered them up the slope into the black jungle. They slogged another hundred yards, slipping and falling in the wet growth, hacking with a machete at vines and branches, and then ran into a patrol of main-force North Vietnamese troops. Thompson was on point, but this night they were hit from behind. He remembered the ferocious hammering of the Vietnamese AK-47s, their noise obliterating all other senses. Trees went down and they could see the sky. Stars glittered. Clouds took the silvery color of the moon. Abruptly, the sky turned white, then a deep blue-black, then white again. Men screamed in two languages. And suddenly the battle was over and Thompson was alone.

He remembered the colossal silence. He remembered thinking, *They're all dead, every fucking one of them, the entire fucking patrol, and I'm alone.* He couldn't see the others. He heard no orders from Hearns. He moved softly, slithering through wet earth, and then saw Barker on his side next to a banyan tree, the back of his head blown off. Thompson felt a throbbing in his leg and reached down and his hand came away wet with blood. *Jesus, I'm shot.* But he was alive, jammed between two fallen trees, with the dead Barker behind him. *Shot in the leg, lots of fucking blood . . .* Thompson lay there, hearing unseen men speaking Vietnamese in soft musical tones. He gripped his M-16, ready to fight, and probably to die.

Now, twenty years later in a pachinko parlor in Tokyo, the memory of that night brought fear pounding through Thompson's body. He remembered waiting a long silent hour (*maybe it was less, maybe it was twenty minutes, maybe it was thirty seconds, there was no time, no clocks, no fragments of days and weeks and months and years, there was only the steady throbbing in my fucking leg*) before sliding out from the protection of the logs, dragging the leg behind him, shards of white blinding pain shooting up the left side of his body. *I smelled shit everywhere, the shit of the wounded, the shit of the dead, the endless foul shit of Vietfuckingnam.* He remembered cocking the M-16. He remembered the fading sound of Vietnamese voices, like bird song, like bamboo striking bamboo, and someone groaning and then a shot and then silence. He slithered along, moving back toward the river and the boat. Somewhere, away off, he heard the rumble of artillery. That was strange, the pounding of a different place, a different war. Here, on the ground near this black river, he was afraid that his own thumping heart would betray him. Behind him in the inky darkness, he heard another pistol shot, fainter, a snapping sound like a fire cracker. *They're shooting the wounded.* He lay still. *They're walking around now shooting the fucking wounded and soon they'll come to me.* He heard movement in the dark, very close, men walking without caution, the way soldiers walk when they've won. Then silence. Then more movement. Then a long silence. He thought: *An animal, some poor goddamned animal, had to be some rabbit or muskrat.* And then, his leg aching, the blood wet: *Or it's one of the guys from the platoon, one of us, wounded, a guy I have to bring with me.* He waited a long time then but heard nothing and was afraid to speak a word. After a long silence, he moved again, using the M-16 like a crutch to shove himself along, dragging the ruined leg behind him.

Then he saw the river. Black and glossy. And off to the side, where they'd left it under some mangrove trees, was the boat.

Thompson paused, listening for the Vietnamese, then moved again. The boat was before him. He would climb in and escape. He reached for it, hauling the bloodied leg.

And then was hit hard in the face.

He rolled, a billion points of pain exploding in his brain, and then looked up.

Hearns was standing above him, his M-16 aimed at Thompson's head. The sergeant smiled and then backed up and stepped into the boat.

"Fuck you, Thompson," he whispered, before using an oar to shove off into the river. He was gone before Thompson could recover enough to shoot him.

The rest of it was luck and pain. Thompson lay one entire day and night on the river bank before an American patrol boat came along. He told the commander, a fresh-faced ensign, what had happened. They recovered the bodies of the destroyed platoon. The ensign called ahead, asking for the arrest of Sergeant Hearns. But when they all reached the base he discovered that Sergeant Hearns had not been arrested. Sergeant Hearns had never been seen again.

It was assumed by the clerks of the battalion that Hearns was dead, shot down by the Vietnamese somewhere else that night, and his name was added to the list of the MIAs. And Thompson remembered thinking, *You won, motherfucker. I was coming back to get you, but you won.*

For Thompson, of course, the war was over. He was flown to a hospital in Japan where they put steel rods in his leg and gave him a plastic kneecap and shot him up with a lot of morphine. The Japanese doctors were kind; the nurses were sweet. When he came out of his drug dreams, he began to read, plunging into Zen as a means of emptying memory, then looking at the life immediately around him. *And where was my Japanese Catherine Barkley? I had made my farewell to arms, without a hard night's journey across Lake Como: but where was the woman who would heal my heart?* And then for the first time he began to learn the language and history of the nation he would study for the rest of his life. He tried hard to think about the world ahead of him, not that filthy world he'd left behind, never again the dark romance of a Hemingway war. There were even some days when he didn't think about Sergeant Hearns.

Eventually Thompson's smashed leg healed, although his heart took longer. But he did get on with his life. He earned a master's degree in Japanese studies and a Ph.D. from Columbia and began to teach. The war ended. He married, fathered two daughters, was divorced. Living alone in an apartment in Miami, he would watch the television news in the evenings and sometimes see rallies for the MIAs. He knew these were cynical exercises, run by slick hustlers who knew that the Vietnamese had no reason to keep prisoners. But some part of him wanted at least one MIA to come out of the jungles alive.

And here he was: across the room, playing pachinko in Tokyo.

Thompson trembled.

And then rose. He went around the side of the machines, and walked in his stiff-legged way down the aisle where Hearns was seated. At the machine beside Hearns, there was a young Japanese kid, dressed in the pink-streaked hair and earrings of the local punks.

"Hello, sergeant," Thompson said.

Hearns looked up, his eyes suddenly wide. His mouth opened, as if he wanted to say something. Thompson saw the yellowing teeth of a heavy smoker. And in the old man's coarse face, the eyes were terrified.

"It's me. Thompson."

Suddenly, Hearns whirled, kicking Thompson in the stomach. He knocked over the young Japanese punk and rushed to the door. Thompson gasped, inhaled deeply, saw Hearns in the street and went after him.

They ran through the snow, which was falling more heavily now: the squat, thickly built American pursued by the taller, younger one with the game leg. Hearns cut into the serene grounds of a temple where snow was gathering on tiled rooftops. He bumped into an old woman, bounced off three young schoolgirls, ducked past a *ramen* shop into an alley. People shouted after him in anger. And then came Thompson. Breathing hard, heaving, a pain in his side, forcing his bad leg to do what it had not done in many years.

Hearns seemed to know where he was going. He dodged into narrow streets, then turned into a maze of blind lanes. He moved through one side of a restaurant and went out the other. But Thompson kept coming. Finally, Hearns burst into a wider street. Before and below him was the Sumida River, a subway station, bridges, stairs leading to a park along the edge of the river. He hurried into the park, as if planning to escape the way he had on another river long ago. He was at the edge, gazing into the oily water, when Thompson caught him.

"You son of a bitch," Thompson said, jerking him around by the collar and then smashing him in the face with his right hand. Hearns fell to his knees and Thompson put his weight on the good leg and kicked him over with the leg from Vietnam. The snow was coming at an angle now, driven by a hard wind, obliterating the city. They were absolutely alone. Hearns crouched on his hands and knees. He ran a hand over his mouth and then took it away, seeing a thin film of blood.

He turned to Thompson.

"What do you want?" he said in a hoarse, beaten voice.

"The truth," Thompson said. "The fucking *truth*. Why'd you leave me there that night? Where'd you go? And how'd you get *here*? I want the whole fucking story, Hearns."

"I don't know what you're talking about. My name is Eddie Duffy. I never saw you before in my life."

Thompson stared at him for a long moment, thinking: *What if he's telling the truth? What if this is not Hearns? Suppose . . .*

Then Hearns was up, scrambling, starting to run. Thompson grabbed him again, and began to punch him in a grunting fury, as the snow fell in the vast, white, empty park and the horn of a riverboat blared mournfully. Hearns went down again and stayed down.

"Tell me the truth," Thompson screamed, his face an inch away from Hearns, "or I'll throw you in the fucking river."

Hearns turned away, his huge body suddenly soft, lying on his back in the snow and mud. He took a cigarette from a pack and snapped a lighter with a shaking hand. He made a thin whimpering sound as he inhaled. *I can't even hit him again*, Thompson thought. *My hands hurt so bad I can't throw another punch.*

"I was sick of the war," Hearns said, staring up at the falling snow. "Sick of the killing. Sick of being afraid, all day, all night. I was even sick of sending assholes like you into villages to kill people I didn't know . . . Everybody knew by then, the war meant nothing. Not a thing. They were all dying for nothing. Our guys and their guys . . . All bullshit. And we could never win it. Never, unless we killed every fucking one of them . . ."

He sat up, took a deep pull on the cigarette and then stared off at the snow falling into the river. His face was lumpy from Thompson's punches. His left eye was closing.

"Remember that time I asked you all to kill everybody in some fucking VC village someplace? Remember that?"

"I never forgot it," Thompson said.

"After that, I knew it was over for me," Hearns said. "I couldn't even report you fuckers for insubordination, because what I wanted you to do wasn't legal. But what happened later, that was your fault, too, Thompson. The day you wouldn't kill everyone in the village, you showed me the truth about the fucking war and I hated you for it and wanted you dead." He flicked the butt into the swirling snow. "The army was my life," he said. "But that day the war ended for me. If I couldn't kill everybody, then I couldn't kill anybody. You said no and killed me as a fucking soldier. I just had to wait for a moment to get away."

"Even if it meant killing me."

Hearns looked blankly at Thompson. "Yeah. Of course. I mean, if it was your ass or my ass, then it was gonna be your ass, soldier."

He stood up.

"How'd you get *here*?"

"None of your fuckin' business," Hearns said.

"Maybe the Japanese cops can decide whose business it is."

"Hey, I'm *legal*, man," Hearns said, with some heat. "I've got papers. I've got a wife here, three kids, a job . . . You can't . . ."

His voice dribbled away. He probably did have a life in Tokyo; it even included pachinko.

"You're a deserter, Hearns," Thompson said. "I'd bet your papers aren't in your name. I bet—"

"All right," Hearns said. "Stop."

The snow felt icier now. Thompson shivered and then saw that Hearns was crying.

"All those fucking dead people," Hearns said, his voice rising and falling with emotion. "Men and women and kids. Our guys. Their guys. All for shit." He turned to Thompson. "And you know what? I don't give a rat's ass anymore. I'm sick of being on the run. I'm sick of hiding. Sick of my fake name and my fake horseshit history. You want me, Thompson? You got me. Come on. Let's go. We'll go to the Jap cops. We'll go to the fucking embassy. Let them know who I really am and get it over with, man."

Thompson stared at him, struggling against pity, thinking. *To hell with it, it was a long time ago, forget about it, say goodbye and leave him alone . . .* He took out his own cigarettes and started to light one.

Suddenly he was down.

And Hearns was running: into the snow, into the blur, into the past, heading for the snowy blank of the Sumida River.

Thompson rose on unsteady legs, stunned, his jaw throbbing, thinking: *Just when I go soft on you, just when I feel sorry for you, you son of a bitch . . .* He watched Hearns go, but he did not follow. The snow was falling steadily on Tokyo. Thompson shivered in the cold until he could no longer see Hearns and then he turned, to face the great snow-silenced city, thinking: *It's over. I don't fucking believe it. The war is over at last.*

Happy New Year

1

At thirty-eight, Hardeman thought his life was splendid. The beginning had been bumpy, of course; he had cried himself to sleep the night he was turned down for a reporter's job at *The New York Times*. But he had risen in the morning and gone on to serve his apprenticeship, covering fires and murders for a New York tabloid, laboring on the foreign desk of a wire service, reporting on two wars and three presidents. And here he was, the Tokyo bureau chief for an American weekly newsmagazine, which was no small thing in his chosen profession. There seemed no limits to the fear, fury, resentment and curiosity of Americans about Japan, so virtually every story he filed was printed, with the usual elisions, corrections and literary barbarisms added by the gnomes in New York. He was proud—some said *too* proud—of his accomplishments. He had written seven cover stories in eighteen months, while his predecessor managed only three in the previous four years. He placed the mash notes from his editors on the bulletin board above his desk, alongside mushy fan letters from American politicians and toadying notes from the chairman of each of the Big Three car companies, lobbying for a level playing field in his coverage of the Japanese auto industry. After his last cover story, four publishers had offered him book contracts, and for the first time in his career he was forced to hire an agent.

Hardeman's growing prestige was best measured by another glittering accomplishment: he had been on "Nightline" four times. This impressed people in Tokyo, where many America-watchers saw "Nightline" on cable; it positively delighted his editors, as proof of

their genius in selecting Hardeman for the bureau, and encouraged
the agent to bargain even harder on his behalf during those long
power lunches at the Four Seasons in New York. There were, of
course, many other indices of Hardeman's success in life and art.
For one thing, he lived better than most Japanese company presidents. The magazine paid for his twelfth floor two-bedroom furnished apartment in a high rise in Hiroo (where he had three telephone lines and a personal fax machine), and he charged off as
expenses most of the other costs of living in Tokyo. He was on the
list for every diplomatic and government reception. He dined in the
best restaurants. He saw the best theater. He drove an excellent car.
And most astonishing of all, he lived with a beautiful woman.

Her name was Noriko. And he was as shocked as his friends and
underlings when he fell in love with her. He often told them that he
didn't think he was ready for another woman. He didn't think he
would ever be ready. The friends all knew the story of how, a few
months before he arrived in Tokyo, his marriage had ended in terrible scenes, complete with slashing dialogue and slammed doors. He
said, with pride that was close to vanity, that he remained civilized
only for the sake of his daughter Kathy, who was twelve. His wife
Sandra, so fresh and exuberant and innocent in her twenties, had
turned mean and possessive and jealous in her thirties. Or so
Hardeman told anyone who asked. She was jealous of his status, he
said, his growing fame, his freedom to travel, above all of his profession, which she called "your goddamned mistress." When he was
asked to cover the People's Power revolution that brought Cory
Aquino to power in the Philippines, Sandra rammed the refrigerator with the palm of her hand and said, "Not again! You just got
back!" She reminded him that because he was always gone *she* had
to meet with all of Kathy's teachers, *she* had to take the child to
movies and museums, *she* had to pay the bills and answer the
phones . . . "And what do *you* do? You *run off*!"

He went to the Philippines anyway. And when the revolution was
over, so was the marriage. His reporting from Manila was brilliant;

it was crucial to delivering to him the bureau chief's job in Tokyo. But when he came home, stopping first at the main office in New York to take the deserved applause, he felt that Sandra had become a kind of black hole. She said nothing, just stared at the wall in a deep and awful depression, smothering his excitement; she finally said that she hadn't read his stories and didn't care if she ever did, and Hardeman knew that if he fell into that black hole with her he would never climb out. As a reporter it was his often uneasy duty to pry out the secrets of other people's lives; now he had to face the facts of his own. His marriage had disintegrated. He waited that night for Kathy to fall asleep and then he told Sandra that he wanted out. She accused him of self-absorption and indifference and unspeakable cruelty. But then she grew quiet and admitted she had already seen a lawyer. And within days, he was presented with the usual bill: alimony and child support and the equal division of community property. Hardeman signed the papers, packed his books for storage, kissed his daughter goodbye and fled.

All of this came out late at night, drinking with the other correspondents at the bar of the Foreign Press Club in Yurakucho. Sometimes he would tell his companions that the reporter's trade was just not compatible with marriage. All were scarred from the marriage wars; they would nod gravely and order another round. Even later at night, back home and reading the faxed stories from the U.S. dailies (for Hardeman was no drunk), he would think: Perhaps I simply have no talent for it. Maybe marriage is an arcane art, he thought, like etching or basket weaving. If it is, then I just don't have the basic God-given skills and like millions of other American men, I might be incapable of learning them.

But Hardeman was also a man; he needed women. For the first six months in Tokyo, he dated in an unplanned, careful, even cautious way. A visiting Belgian fashion model. The twice-divorced correspondent for a Canadian television network. A teacher from an English-language school. Some others he could not categorize in the shorthand of the journalist; they passed quickly across the screen before he pushed "delete." The sex was usually good, possibly, he thought, *because* there were no emotional commitments or demands. If a demand appeared, if a woman's eyes glazed over with the possibility of a commitment, Hardeman's passion ebbed, his erection vanished, he prepared his escape. In that strategy, the job always helped. He would assign himself to cover the student movement in Korea or some biochemical experiment in Okinawa or spring training in Kyushu and when he got back and spent a few more days ducking phone calls, the woman would understand and go away. He soon began to feel like what used to be called A Confirmed Bachelor. And he enjoyed it. He felt younger, more flexible, more *worldly* than he'd ever felt in his life. Then, at a packed government press conference announcing resignations caused by one of the periodic big business payoff scandals, he met Noriko.

They found themselves standing together at the press bar, contending for the services of the bartender. He bowed and waved a hand and she smiled back and ordered a ginger ale. He asked for the same, then offered a mock toast: "To bigger and better government scandals!" She said, "It's getting so you can use the same story every two months and just change the names." He said, "Sometimes you don't even have to change the names." She laughed. Then as she turned, he said: "Excuse me, but would you like to have dinner?" And she said, "Why not?"

And so they did. She was thirty, single, a free-lance producer of television shows and coordinator of special events for American networks. When the Emperor died, she helped set up the coverage for one of those networks, choosing the best spots to place cameras, locating English-speaking experts on Japanese culture and history, obtaining all the necessary permits. Her English was impeccable, learned in a Catholic intermediate school in Tokyo, polished by three years in an American university. She was cool under pressure. She had a good sense of humor. And she didn't want to get married. In short, she was perfect.

"You think *you* have no talent for marriage?" she said to Hardeman on their third date. "I have even less."

Three months later, she moved in with him. She did not, however, give up her own small apartment in Aoyama. "In this life," she said with a laugh, "nothing is forever."

But from the first day, she changed the way he lived. She started with the apartment, moving furniture to create more space, adding lamps for light, changing curtains, arranging for the delivery of fresh flowers every few days, making it a bright open place instead of a chilly high-rise aerie with the atmosphere of a hotel. Before Noriko's arrival, Hardeman used the second bedroom for storage, stacking it with unopened boxes of books and old files. Noriko ordered bookcases and a file cabinet and made him empty the cartons. She bought a table for his computer (upon which he could write his book) and a smaller one for the fax machine (which had been perched on a sideboard beside the candelabra) and turned the room into a home office. She framed some of his cover stories and placed them on the walls of the bathroom, along with photographs of Hardeman in Managua and Afghanistan and even in high school. Later he realized how shrewdly Noriko had read the text of his vanity; every time he took a leak his progress in the world was validated by the evidence of those walls.

Without any obvious effort, she also made his life smoother. In addition to the flower deliveries, she arranged for a service to pick up and deliver his laundry, another to keep his suits and his shoes in perfect condition, a third to clean the apartment twice a week. When she first opened his bachelor's refrigerator, she laughed out loud; it looked like an abandoned lot. She went shopping and filled the shelves with fresh fruit and vegetables, mineral water, and the basics of some decent meals, creating a green and colorful oasis in the kitchen. Then, to be sure it was always replenished, she found a grocery store that would deliver if she placed an order by fax. She bought good plates and cups, bowls and saucers, stacking them in an artful way, storing those that came with the lease in some dark corner of the basement. She found a set of place mats from Singapore to add color to the teak table. She came in one afternoon with spices and sauces whose names he'd never heard before, and with almost no effort she cooked a superb dinner, all the while talking and joking about politics and scandals and Hardeman's latest assignment. She didn't cook every night; they were both too busy. But every Saturday night, after his last piece of copy had been filed to New York, they made a ritual of a sumptuous meal at home.

Her presence in his life was not just a concert in domestic skills. She forced him to read the newspapers out loud, correcting his dreadful Japanese. She brought him suggestions for stories and even arranged some interviews from her own superb network of contacts and sources. She knew all the gossip from the halls of power: which minister had a girlfriend stashed in an apartment in the Ginza, which middle-level functionary at MITI was caught making a private deal in Eastern Europe, which old company boss was planning to cut off the inheritance to his alcoholic son. Unlike Hardeman, who took seriously the affairs of power, she laughed at their essential absurdity. When he grew too grim or sour, or too swollen with self-importance, she laughed and took him to bed. She taught him many things there too.

She did all of this without missing a beat in her own career. When he had to fly off to the Philippines to cover still another coup attempt against the Aquino government, or to Taiwan to analyze the decline of the Chiang family, she wished him good luck, asked him to telephone when he had time, and went off, as always, to her own work. She treated him like a man and a professional, not a territory to be possessed. And when he returned, she was warm and loving and exciting in bed.

"I think I'm in love with you," he said one evening.

"Don't even say that word again until you're sure," she said. "Besides, I don't want any of this 'I think' stuff. . . ." She laughed and pinched his cheek and added: "And you'd better tell me in Japanese."

2

One morning, traveling to his office in the Ginza on the Hibiya line, he began thinking about an article comparing the Tokyo subways to the wretched system in New York. He hurried up to the office, full of enthusiasm.

There were two other reporters in the bureau: Mac, who covered economics, Susan, who backed up Hardeman with research and translations, and Sachiko. Hardeman couldn't truly describe Sachiko's function; it involved everything. She had started at the magazine in 1951, when she was nineteen; now she was a grandmother, and ran the small office as if it were an extension of her maternal duties.

Without effort, she made certain that the coffeepot was always full, the newspapers always displayed on Hardeman's desk, the important stories marked with an orange felt-tip marker, the schedule of the day's press events neatly typed. She sorted out the telephone messages. She made appointments. She handled all of the expenses and the fax traffic back and forth to New York. In almost forty years on the job, she had seen bureau chiefs come and go and had no known emotional attachment to any of them. She was committed only to the magazine and the private, unknown terrain of her own life.

On this morning, with Mac and Susan out on assignments, Sachiko looked up as Hardeman came in and handed him some phone messages. And then, without any shift in her neutral tone, she added:

"And, oh, yes, your wife called from the States. She said it was urgent."

"Urgent?"

"That's what she said," Sachiko repeated, as if not believing for a moment that such a call could ever be urgent.

He went into his office and dialed the old number. Sandra answered. There was no small talk.

"It's Kathy. I can't handle her anymore. Ever since you left, she's never been the same, she's in terrible shape, I think she's getting in trouble at school here, they're all smoking pot, and maybe sleeping around, and she's only thirteen, and boys call here all the time, day and night, not boys, but *men*, with deep voices like men and . . ."

"Slow down," Hardeman said, wondering: how did I ever love her? What was it?

"And I can't handle her," Sandra went on, the connection so perfect he thought she might be in Tokyo. "She won't listen to me, she just does what she *wants*. I tell her to stay home and she goes out, and I don't know where she is, and last night, no, the night before, I don't know, the other night—she stayed out *all night*, said she was at some girlfriend's house, but I knew she was lying and I don't know what to do. The summer vacation starts next week and that'll be worse and I can't keep track of her and it's because of *you*, goddamnit, she blames me for the breakup, she thinks it's *my* goddamned fault you split, she, she—"

"Calm down."

"Calm down? *Calm down?* This is your *daughter*, goddamnit! This is little Kathy! Our daughter! And you haven't lived here for a long time now, and there's *crack* around now, all over the goddamned place, and she doesn't know what she's doing and they have teenagers getting AIDS now too and she might get pregnant and right now, it's the middle of the night here, and I don't even know where she *is*, she might be sleeping with six guys, she might—"

"Hold it, hold it," Hardeman said. "I'm six thousand miles away, Sandra. What do you want me to do about it?"

A silence. Then:

"Take her."

"What?"

"Take her to Tokyo."

"You're kidding," Hardeman said.

"No, I'm not. I mean it. Take her there, put her in school. I'll give up the child support. She'll have you, she'll have discipline. . . . I'm always reading about how goddamned disciplined those Japanese schools are and—"

She seemed to run down then. Hardeman waited, his stomach churning with indecision. He glanced at the desk photograph of Kathy when she was eight years old. He was holding her hand, the two of them squinting into the sun on a vacation beach in Acapulco. And an image of Noriko rose in his mind, walking into his kitchen in a white bathrobe, blowsy with morning.

"I'll think about it," Hardeman said. "And call you back."

3

On a hot Sunday in July, he went alone to meet his daughter at the airport in Narita. He was anxious to see her now, even happy; she would be here for a year and he would have to adjust his life again. But he felt confident that he could make it work. Noriko would do it. Noriko could make anything work.

When Kathy came out of the baggage area, he saw immediately that she had changed. She was taller, her legs longer, her face more clearly defined. She had breasts now too, and knew that young men looked at her when she walked. She glanced around in a tentative way, and then saw him in the crowd and smiled and hurried to him.

"Oh, Daddy," she said. "I missed you so much."

"And I missed you too," he said.

But the smile soon vanished and she was oddly silent as he drove the long road from the airport to Tokyo. He thought she must be jet-lagged, but when he glanced over, her eyes were wide open.

"You okay?" he said.

"Sure."

"Why so quiet?"

"I don't know. Maybe I'm just quiet, that's all."

She watched the grungy industrial landscape in a dull way and showed enthusiasm only once. "Hey," she said, "that looks like Disneyland!"

He laughed. "That *is* Disneyland."

"In Japan?"

"In Japan," he said. "We'll take you some time."

"We?"

"Noriko and I."

"Is that a girl's name?"

"Yes. But she's a woman."

"And she lives with you?"

"With us," Hardeman said.

"I see."

Kathy didn't say another word until they reached the apartment. In the basement garage, she pointed at a sign in *kanji*.

"What do all those squiggles mean?" she said.

"The same things that our little squiggles mean," Hardeman said. "No smoking. Or compact cars only. Or don't leave your keys. Mysterious things like that."

"You can read them?"

"Some of them. I'm still learning."

"She's teaching you?"

"She helps."

Noriko was away at her office when they entered the apartment, but she had done her best to adjust to the new arrangement. There was a bed in Hardeman's office now, and a bureau, and hangers in the closet. The computer had been packed up and taken to the magazine, the bookcase moved into the living room to make more space in what was now Kathy's room.

"It's pretty small," she said, as he laid her suitcases on the bed. She looked down the hall, past the bathroom, to the open door of the master bedroom.

"She sleeps with you in there?" Kathy said.

"Yes."

There was a pause, and then she whispered: "I see."

4

The war against Noriko began that night. Hardeman was at the head of the table, Kathy to his right, Noriko to his left. Noriko had prepared a simple Japanese meal, with sashimi and rice and green tea. But even after a long afternoon nap, Kathy seemed inert. She stared at the food.

"I can't eat this," she said.

"How come?"

"I hate raw fish."

Noriko smiled. "I keep reading that Americans now eat more sushi and sashimi than the Japanese."

"I hate it," the girl said, her face pouting.

"What would you rather have?" Hardeman said.

"A Big Mac."

Noriko laughed. "Okay. Your father and I will eat this and later we'll go out and find you a Big Mac."

"They have Big Macs here?"

"Hundreds of them," Noriko said. "Thousands. Millions."

"I bet they're disgusting," the girl said.

Noriko glanced at Hardeman, her look saying: what's this?

"It depends on your taste," Hardeman said. "I never cared for Big Macs, even back home."

Without a word, Kathy got up and went to her room and closed the door. Noriko looked at Hardeman.

"It's okay," she said in a calm way. "It will just take some patience. She's a kid."

But it wasn't okay. After dinner, they went out and found a McDonald's and bought the girl a Big Mac and some french fries. They were, Kathy said, disgusting. "They don't know how to do anything here," she said. When Hardeman told her to learn a little more about Japan before venting her opinions, the girl sulked. Hardeman felt a chill in the July air.

That night, as Hardeman and Noriko tried to sleep, the girl kept moving around the apartment. She went to the bathroom a dozen times, opening and closing the door loudly, running water in the sink, flushing the toilet. Once, Hardeman heard a sound outside the door, as if she were standing there, listening. He got up angrily, pulled on a bathrobe, opened the door. Nobody was there. But Noriko was now awake.

"Jet lag," she whispered. "Come to sleep . . ."

But in the weeks that followed, the tension grew. Hardeman had enrolled Kathy in an international school in Roppongi, filled with the children of foreign businessmen and diplomats. That kept her occupied most of the day. But she started calling Hardeman at the bureau, complaining about teachers, classmates, the difficulty of learning Japanese, the cliques of older children. And in the evenings, the hostility to Noriko deepened. She made it clear that she hated Japanese food, wouldn't even try it. When asked to help set the table and wash the dishes, she acted as if this were some cruel form of punishment. She talked about her mother as if Noriko wasn't there, chatting in a brittle way about her mother's clothes and what her mother had to say about politics and music and schools. She often drifted around the apartment with a Walkman plugged into her skull, moving to music they couldn't hear, sending the message that she found Noriko's conversation worthless. She threw her clothes in dirty piles on the floor of her room, forcing Noriko to pick them up. She received a letter from the States, and retreated in silence behind her door, as if to contemplate a precious treasure. But when Noriko asked her later: "Good news from home?" she sneered and said, "None of your business."

Then one evening, Hardeman came home and at the dinner table (sushi for the grown-ups, pizza for Kathy) told them that he had to go to Seoul in the morning. "I've been waiting for three months for this interview," he said. "I'll be back the next day."

"You can't go!" Kathy said.

"It's my job, honey."

"Then take me with you."

Noriko said, "Your father's a professional, Kathy. He can't bring people with him when he's working."

Kathy ignored this and said to her father: "You can't leave me alone with *her*."

Noriko got up from the table and went into the kitchen and Hardeman looked at Kathy and thought: You are your mother's daughter now, all right. I used to think you were mine, and you were, but not anymore.

But the next morning, he went off alone to Seoul. Noriko went to work and Kathy went to school. That night, Noriko dined alone in the kitchen, telling Kathy she could help herself to some corn flakes. Then Noriko went into the bedroom and closed the door. She lay down in her clothes. She smoked cigarettes. She watched television with the sound off. And then the door opened. Kathy walked in, gazing around the bedroom and down at Noriko.

"Is he a good lover?" the girl said. Noriko ignored her. "What does he do to you in that bed?" Noriko lit another cigarette. "What do you do to him?"

Noriko stared at the girl for a long moment and then said: "Get out of this room. Now."

The next day, when Hardeman returned from Seoul, Noriko packed her things and moved back to her old apartment.

5

Weeks passed, then months. In these days of her triumph, Kathy seemed more and more happy. She still received her weekly letter, and read it in solemn privacy. But she made some friends at school. She started writing a very basic Japanese. She ate sashimi when Hardeman took her to restaurants. She discovered that she loved *ramen*. She watched television, repeating the words in Japanese, and began decoding the dialogue in the Japanese comic books.

But Hardeman was miserable. The agent had arranged a book deal with a fat advance but Hardeman kept postponing the work.

Everywhere he looked in the apartment, from the arrangement of the pictures in the bathroom to the contents of the refrigerator, he saw Noriko. He tried to remember the blissful months they'd spent together, when work and life were seamless and happy; they seemed long ago now. Occasionally, he called her for some piece of information, the name of a source, some elaboration on a story; she was friendly but correct; Noriko never flirted. He even had a few cool lunches with her and twice she invited him to dinner parties at her apartment; each time, there were friends present and he went home alone. She was very clear: she would not take part in a war with Kathy for Hardeman's affections. "I'm too old for that," she said in a cool way. "It uses up too much energy."

In his work, Hardeman put in long hours, many of them at home, but his old buoyant egotism had ebbed. He took down the fawning letters from the bulletin board. He removed the photographs from the walls in the john, those trophies of his career, and packed them into a box and stashed them in the basement storage room. He did "Nightline" again, but didn't even mention it at lunch with his friends at the Press Club. Thinking about Kathy, he thought back on his marriage to Sandra, and came to a conclusion that would have been impossible even six months earlier: I was an asshole. Once that sentence entered his mind, its corollary appeared: I *am* an asshole. One afternoon, instead of outlining his book, or reading the Japanese magazines or the handouts from the government offices, he wrote down words on yellow pads, describing himself: self-absorbed, insufferable, vain, selfish, ruthless. Yes, ruthless. A ruthless asshole. Remembering moves he had made in the eternal games of career politics. Remembering sly betrayals of colleagues during tense lunches with his superiors, saying *Great guy but drinks too much* or *If he worked a little harder he'd be great* or *He was my hero but he's in a kind of a slump, isn't he?* Remembering the way he forgot two wedding anniversaries because he was off on assignments and how he couldn't even get to see Kathy in her eighth grade class play because there was a heavy meeting at the magazine and he didn't want to give the impression that anything was more important than his work. And remembering women he'd fucked and forgotten.

He was sure Noriko must have seen all of this in him. She saw everything else. She must have seen him for what he was. After living with him a while. Of course. That's why she really left, wasn't it? Not Kathy. Me. And who could blame her? Why would any woman want to live with such an impossible asshole? Then, deprived of much of his vanity—and its brother, certainty—he wanted her more than ever, wanted to live with her without all that baggage, at last relieved of the heavy load of self. He could stop preening, stop exulting, and start living. She would see him for what he was. She would love him for that. But the journalist in him kept stepping back, looking objectively at the facts, and he understood that it could never work. If he could convince Noriko of his transformation, if she would accept it, if they got married and she moved back to the apartment, Kathy's adolescent furies would return. If he began to do things for Noriko the way she had done things for him, Kathy would rise in cold and vengeful revolt. She would try to destroy Noriko and the marriage. And Hardeman thought: I can't do that, I can't walk Noriko into that minefield.

So he dated other women and slept with some of them. He did this, he believed, in the same objective way that he had assessed the situation with Noriko. With these women he risked nothing, performing as if he were going to some gymnasium; that was being an asshole, true, but what the hell: maybe that's what I am, now and forever. Maybe that's the way of most of the human race. On those evenings when he came home late, Kathy said nothing. No complaints. No petty jealous pouts. It was as if she understood that with Noriko gone, she had no genuine rival for her father's affections. Women were not a threat; a woman was. She had won.

Slowly he began to work on his book, skipping the receptions, avoiding the theater, staying out of the Press Club. But alone in the dark, Hardeman still ached for Noriko. One night, unable to sleep, he called her and asked if he could come over. But she whispered in a sweet cool voice, "I'm sorry, there's somebody here." That night Hardeman cried for the first time in fifteen years.

Still, he made no attempt to erase her from his memory, like some old failed story in the computer. At Christmas he bought her a lovely watch and a book about Giotto. She agreed to meet him for dinner in a Chinese restaurant in Roppongi. He got there early and she arrived a half hour late, smiling her apologies. She told him she loved the book on Giotto, he was one of her favorites, he reminded her of Diego Rivera, the Mexican, the same crowded compositions, the same patterns, and she said it would be delicious someday to live in Florence where so many of the paintings were still on the walls of churches and chapels. He started to say that he would take her there, and then cut himself short; she can afford to go herself, she knows how to travel, she doesn't need me. Shut up, he thought; don't be an asshole. She had some Christmas presents for him too: a sweater and some leather gloves and a matching Mont Blanc pen and pencil set. He did little doodles on a napkin, first with the pen, then the pencil, and then took her small soft hand.

"I want you to come back," he said quietly.

"I can't," she said. "You know that better than I do. It would destroy us both."

He paused, and then said in Japanese, "I love you."

She smiled, but tears were welling in her eyes.

"I want to marry you, Noriko."

She reached for a glass of water, glanced around the crowded restaurant.

"No," she said. "Not now."

6

On New Year's Eve, as he lay alone in bed, Sandra called.

"Happy New Year," he said.

"Don't be sarcastic," she said. "Is Kathy there?"

"Hold on."

He got up, turned off the sound, pulled on a robe, and went to Kathy's room.

"It's your mother."

Kathy looked puzzled. She went into his bedroom to the telephone and Hardeman walked to the kitchen and opened an iced bottle of Kirin beer. He looked out over the bright lights of the great city, which for a short while he had loved even more than his own. Out there, somewhere, Noriko was getting on with her life, drifting farther and farther out of his. Eventually, she would meet someone and fall in love, and the man would love her back and then she'd be gone forever. Just like that. It happens to lots of people. Fuck it: another year was starting, another segment of time. I will publish a book this year, he thought, but I feel no elation. In a way, I don't care. There is no steadily rising line in my mind now, no inevitable ascent to the heights, no certainty that if I do everything right, I will end up at the top of the magazine, top of the profession. He sipped the cold beer. In the building across the way, he saw a group of Westerners at a party, complete with funny hats from home. In the future, he would cover wars and revolutions, great conferences and small disasters; he would sleep with strange women; he would get old and talk too much about the years when he was young. He would stay away from Tokyo.

He heard a murmur from the bedroom, but no distinct words. And then, as he finished the beer, Kathy came in, her voice shaking, tears in her eyes.

"Mom wants to talk to you," she said. "She wants me to come home."

He went into the bedroom, closing the door behind him, and picked up the phone.

"Are you nuts?" he said. "She's just getting settled, she's making friends, she—"

"I want her," Sandra said. "She's mine. It says so in the divorce papers."

"Fuck the divorce papers! She's *here*. Going to school. You can't—"

Then a small wire of hysteria came into Sandra's voice.

"What I told you? remember? About her getting wild and all that? I didn't tell you the whole truth. She wasn't in real trouble. It was *me*, me that was in trouble. Yes, she had a boyfriend. A sweet kid, wants to be a poet, writes her letters twenty-seven pages long, just like you used to do. But the truth? I had a boyfriend too. Ten years younger than me, handsome, oh God, a real goddamned Apollo. He was everything you weren't. He's a landscape architect. I don't think he ever read a book in his life, or ever traveled out of the state of New Jersey . . ."

"What is this?" Hardeman said. "*True Confessions?*"

"I'm trying to explain something to you, goddamnit! Will you just *listen?*" He listened. "The thing was, I wanted the guy to move in with us. I wanted him there. I wanted his razor in the bathroom. I wanted a man's smell in the house." A pause. Her voice cracked slightly. Hardeman remembered the way her voice cracked one weekend when they were in college and he told her he'd slept with some psychology major. Long ago. Before they married. "Well, anyway, the guy came for a weekend, with a little bag and all, ready to give it a try. 'Let's roll the dice,' he said to me. You know, trying to be cool. Like he was Frank Goddamned Sinatra or something. And then Kathy went to war against him, she let him know she hated him, that he wasn't as good as you, that he was a dumb kid. I mean, he's *younger* than I am, younger than you, but he's nice, you would've liked him. . . ."

"I'm sure. I always liked gardeners."

"Fuck you," she said. There was a pause, then: "So anyway . . . after Kathy went with you, he moved in, with a suitcase this time," she said. A pause again. He tried to figure out what time it was back home but the numbers kept scrambling. "It didn't work out. I guess maybe I was too old for him, too critical, too hard."

"That part I believe."

"Give it up, will you?" she said. "Anyway, he's gone." Her voice flattened. "And the truth? You want to hear the balls-ass naked truth? I can't stand being alone. I want Kathy back."

"You mean you can't get along without the child support."

"That's a rotten thing to say," she said angrily. "I have a *job* now! And you know it. Teaching. I'm getting *paid*. I don't need—"

Hardeman lowered his voice, cooled his tone. "What if she doesn't want to leave."

"She just told me she did," Sandra said. "She wants her boyfriend back, the kid that writes the letters. She wants to be with her old friends. And she said you—she said she'd been mean and rotten to your woman, whoever the bitch is."

"She isn't a bitch, bitch."

Sandra laughed. He hadn't heard her laugh for more than four years.

"Okay, she isn't a bitch, you asshole."

It was Hardeman's turn to laugh.

"On that, you're right," he said softly. "I have certainly been an asshole."

That calmed her down. The hysteria vanished. Only the need remained. They talked for a while longer, about practical matters, and then hung up. Hardeman stared at the telephone and grew very still, but his heart was beating more quickly. He opened the door and found Kathy sitting on the couch in the living room. He went over and sat on a chair facing her. Her tears had dried.

"Do I have to go?" she said.

"Only if you want to."

She was quiet for a long moment. "You'll be all alone. And that's my fault. I was so terrible to Noriko."

"True."

"I don't want you to be sad, Daddy," she said. "You're such a nice man. I want you to be happy."

"I want you to be happy too, Kathy."

She glanced away, out at the neon signs of the great foreign city, where neon signs spoke in all of those codes that she had not yet cracked.

"Well, the truth of the matter is, I have this boyfriend back home. He's only fifteen, but he's real mature, and he's real smart and—"

An hour later, as the cheap horns of a New Year's midnight punctured the night air, Hardeman was in his car, racing across the darkening city, heading for Aoyama, his heart beating wildly, rehearsing the words of love in Japanese. Be there, he whispered out loud. Please be there. Alone.